L.G. Alexander

PLAIN ENGLISH

INTERMEDIATE

Students' Book

Longman

Contents

Contents

Lesson 1

Help!

Stay there, and be good!

At exactly the same moment, Bertie came out of the newsagent's . . .

Narrator:	Bertie parked the 'Somna-Mobile' (the family motor-caravan) outside a newsagent's and got out. He spoke to his two children, Vicki and Eddie.
Bertie:	I must get a newspaper. Stay there, and be good!
Vicki:	Yes, dad. We're doing a quiz. I've just answered all the questions. Eddie can't answer any of them! Eddie used to help me with quizzes, but he doesn't any more.
Eddie:	That's not fair! You're nine and I'm only six!
Narrator:	Bertie's wife, Fay, was in the back of the Somna. It was 11 o'clock and she wanted to make coffee. She looked out of the window.
Fay:	Ah! There's a supermarket next to that newsagent's. I must get some more coffee.
Narrator:	Fay found some small change. Then she got out of the back door and went into the supermarket. At exactly the same moment, Bertie came out of the newsagent's reading his newspaper. He didn't see Fay. He got into the motor-caravan and drove away!

Talk about the Story!

1   What will Bertie, Vicki and Eddie think when they find Fay isn't there? What will they do?
2   What will Fay think when she finds the Somna isn't there? What will she do?

1

Study!

Used to

1 *We often use* **used to** *instead of the Simple Past when we want to talk about things that are not true any more or do not happen any more.*
I **used to be** a bank clerk, but now I'm a musician.
He **used to work** in a bank, but now he plays in an orchestra.

2 *We often use* **never** *and* **any more** *with* **used to***:*
My father **used to smoke** a lot, but he doesn't smoke **any more**.
My sister **never used to smoke**, but she does now.

3 **REMEMBER!** *There is no present form of* **used to**. *If we want to talk about things that* ALWAYS HAPPEN, *we must use the Simple Present:*
I **always get up** at 7 in the morning.

Listen, Say and Learn!

	I USED TO . . .	BUT NOW I . . .	I'D LIKE TO . . .
I used to	be a civil servant. work in an office. live in London.	am a bank clerk. work in a bank. live in the country.	be a musician. play in an orchestra. live by the sea.

Practise!

1 *Someone is interviewing you for a job.*
Refer to the table above and talk like this:
S1 What do you do now?
S2 I'm a bank clerk.
S1 What did you use to be?
S2 I used to be a civil servant.
S1 What would you really like to be?
S2 I'd really like to be a musician.

2 *About you.*
Make true statements about yourself like this:
S I'm a bank clerk at the moment.
I used to be a civil servant.
I'd really like to be a musician.

Lesson 2

Read . . .

Mind your head!

Look up the word 'headhunter' in a
dictionary and it will probably say
something about tribal wars. But in
modern business, the word describes
5 someone who (for a fee!) finds a good
executive in one firm and offers him
or her a job in another. Headhunters
find out all about you first: who you
are, what you used to do and what you
10 would like to do. Headhunting is big
business, so if you're going places,
mind your head!

Mind your head!

. . . and Answer!

1 What do you think is the original meaning
of 'headhunter'?
2 Is 'headhunter' a good word to use in
modern business? Why/Why not?

3 How do headhunters work in modern
business?
4 Where would you expect to find the
expression 'Mind your head!'?

Listen and Decide!

*You are a headhunter and have just phoned someone for information about Colin Upton, a
young executive who is going places.*

1 *Give the right order of the businesses Colin has been in:*

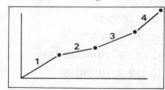

computer company   1 _____   3 _____
bank   _____   _____
advertising firm   2 _____   4 _____
supermarket business   _____   _____

2 *Arrange in order of importance for Colin:*

money   1 _____
power   2 _____
family   3 _____
health   4 _____

3

A Slice of Life

Here are the results of a survey about jobs. People were asked the question:

How satisfied are you with your present job?

More satisfied than average	% satisfied	Less satisfied than average	% satisfied
clergyman	58%	economist	19%
company director	48%	computer programmer	18%
farmer	48%	laboratory assistant	18%
optician	45%	skilled manual jobs (e.g. printer)	18%
solicitor	43%	engineer	17%
primary school teacher	42%	secretary	17%
shopkeeper	42%	management trainee	16%
photographer	41%	unskilled manual jobs	15%
vet	37%	research assistant	14%
actor/musician	36%	draughtsman	8%

Talk about the job survey in class:

1 Why do you think those people doing the jobs listed on the left were 'more satisfied than average'?

2 Why do you think those people doing the jobs listed on the right were 'less satisfied than average'?

3 Which job would you like to do?

"Stop fooling about and take your job seriously"

Writing/Homework

Guided Summary

Read the text on page 3 again. Complete these sentences to describe the job of a 'headhunter' in modern business. Your answer should be in one paragraph of not more than 55 words.

1 A 'headhunter' in modern business is someone who . . .
2 Before he can do this . . .

Composition

Choose one of the jobs listed in A Slice of Life above and write about five sentences saying why you would or would not enjoy it.

Lesson 3

Help!

I'll make some coffee soon!

At exactly the same moment, Fay came out with a jar of coffee . . .

Narrator:	While Fay was in the supermarket, another Somna-Mobile parked outside. The driver spoke to his wife.
Man:	I must get a newspaper.
Woman:	Sorry! What did you say?
Man:	I said I must get a paper. I'll be back in a moment.
Narrator:	The woman nodded and the man went into the newsagent's. At exactly the same moment, Fay came out with a jar of coffee in her hand. She opened the back door of the Somna and got in.
Fay:	I'll make some coffee soon.
Narrator:	. . . she said. Two minutes later the man came out of the shop.
Woman:	Did you buy a paper, dear?
Man:	Yes, my love. We're going to have very nice weather for our holiday.
Woman:	What'll it be like this week?
Man:	Fine and sunny every day.
Narrator:	The man gave the paper to his wife, started the engine and drove away. The woman looked at the paper and said:
Woman:	I'll make some coffee soon.

Talk about the Story!

1 What will the man and the woman think when they find Fay in the back of their Somna? What will they do?
2 What will Fay think when she sees the man and the woman? What will she do?

5

Study! 1

Reported statements with Modal Verbs: Present → Present

Direct statements: _Reported statements:_

He says (that) . . .

I	must	get a newspaper.	he	must	get a newspaper.
I	will	be back soon, but	He	will	be back soon, but
I	may	be half an hour. Then	he	may	be half an hour. Then
we	can	have some coffee.	we	can	have some coffee.

Practise! 1

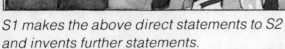

> Tell your mother
> I must get a newspaper.
> I will be back soon, but
> I may be half an hour. Then
> we can have some coffee.

> Dad says (that)
> he must get a newspaper.
> He says he will be back soon, but
> he may be half an hour. Then
> we can have some coffee.

S1 makes the above direct statements to S2
and invents further statements.

S2 reports the message to S3.

Study! 2

Reported statements with Modal Verbs: Present → Past

Direct statements: _Reported statements:_

He said (or told me) (that) . . .

I	must	get a newspaper.	he	must/had to	get a newspaper.
I	will	be back soon, but	He	would	be back soon, but
I	may	be half an hour. Then	he	might	be half an hour. Then
we	can	have some coffee.	we	could	have some coffee.

Practise! 2

Repeat the exercise above with S2 reporting in the past.

Lesson 4

Read . . .

Musical superstar

Andrew Lloyd Webber

By the age of nine, Andrew Lloyd Webber knew he would be a composer. He and Tim Rice (who wrote the lyrics) have created famous musicals like
5 *Evita*. Andrew was born in 1949. His father was Director of the London College of Music. His mother was a famous music teacher. His brother, Julian, is an outstanding cellist.

10 Andrew was already famous when he was twenty. Next time you catch yourself humming *Don't cry for me Argentina*, you'll know who wrote it!

. . . and Choose!

1 By the age of nine, Lloyd Webber
   a) was a composer. b) worked with Tim Rice. c) knew he would compose music.

2 Lloyd Webber probably
   a) heard a lot of music at home. b) met Tim Rice when he was 9. c) wrote *Evita* when he was twenty.

Listen, Choose and Say!

You are listening to a talk on the radio about **Cats***, a famous musical by Andrew Lloyd Webber.*

1 *Choose the right information below:*

The words of *Cats* are by	a) Tim Rice
	b) T.S. Eliot
These words are _____ about cats.	a) comic poems
	b) clever lyrics
The title of the book was	a) *Cats*
	b) *Old Possum's Book of Practical Cats*
They were set to music by Lloyd Webber	a) long after the poet's death
	b) when the poet was still alive
The most famous cat is	a) Possum
	b) Eliot
	c) Macavity
One of the most beautiful songs is called	a) *Cats*
	b) *Memory*

2 *Now refer to the choices you have made and give us a summary of the radio talk.*

A Slice of Life

Here are some of the words of 'Memory' from **Cats**. *A cat remembers her past life.*

Memory

Midnight, not a sound from the pavement.
Has the moon lost her memory?
She is smiling alone.
In the lamp light the withered leaves collect at my feet
And the wind begins to moan.

Memory. All alone in the moonlight
I can smile at the old days.
I was beautiful then.
I remember the time I knew what happiness was,
Let the memory live again.

Every street lamp seems to beat a fatalistic warning
Someone mutters and the street lamp gutters,
And soon it will be morning.

Daylight. I must wait for the sunrise
I must think of a new life
And I mustn't give in.
When the dawn comes tonight will be a memory, too
And a new day will begin.

Burnt-out ends of smoky days
The stale cold smell of morning.
The street lamp dies, another night is over,
Another day is dawning.

Touch me. It's so easy to leave me
All alone with the memory
Of my days in the sun.
If you touch me you'll understand what happiness is.
Look, a new day has begun.

Talk about the poem in class. Say what the words mean for you. Do you like the poem? Why/Why not?

Writing/Homework

Guided Summary

Read the text on page 7 again. Complete these sentences to describe the life of Andrew Lloyd Webber. Your answer should be in one paragraph of not more than 60 words.

1   Andrew Lloyd Webber and Tim Rice have created . . .
2   Andrew was born into a musical family in . . .
3   His father was . . .
4   His mother was . . . and his brother . . .
5   By the time he was twenty, Andrew . . .

Composition

In a few sentences say what the poem 'Memory' is about. Then say whether you like or dislike it and why.

Lesson 5

Help!

That coffee's taking a long time!

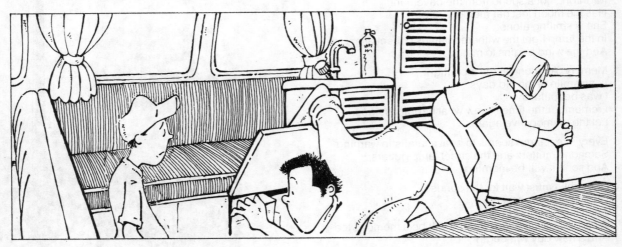

Perhaps she fell out.

Narrator: Bertie suddenly remembered that he wanted some coffee.
Bertie: We needn't stop for coffee. I can drink it at the wheel.
But why is the coffee taking such a long time, Vicki?
What's your mother doing?
Vicki: I'll have a look. Dad! Dad!
Bertie: What's the matter, Vicki?
Vicki: Dad! Mum isn't here!
Bertie: What do you mean 'isn't here'?
Vicki: She isn't here in the back of the Somna!
Narrator: Bertie stopped the motor-caravan suddenly. He and Eddie
hurried into the back. They all looked under the beds,
in the cupboards, in the fridge and in the cooker.
Bertie: Heavens!
Vicki: Perhaps she fell out.
Bertie: What did you say, Vicki?
Vicki: I said perhaps she fell out.
Bertie: Fell out? You mustn't say things like that!
Eddie: I want my mum! I want my mum!

Talk about the Story!

1   Why is it hard for them to explain the absence of Fay?
2   Do you think Fay knows that her family is very worried about her at this moment? Why/Why
    not?

9

Study!

1   Must *and* have to*: NECESSITY*
    We use must *or* have to *to express necessity.*
    This means there is no choice:
    I must stop/He must stop at the red light.
    I have to stop/He has to stop at the red light.

2   Mustn't*: PROHIBITION*
    must *and* have to *usually have the same meaning, but*
    mustn't *and* don't have to *NEVER have the same meaning.*
    We use mustn't *ONLY for prohibition.*
    Mustn't *means we have no choice:*
    You mustn't smoke here. It says 'No Smoking'.

3   Don't have to *and* needn't*: 'IT'S NOT NECESSARY'*
    We use don't have to *or* needn't *when there is a choice:*
    We know they've arrived safely, so we needn't worry.
    We know they've arrived safely, so we don't have to worry.
    I've already checked the bill, so he needn't check it again.
    I've already checked the bill, so he doesn't have to check it again.

Practise!

1
2
3
4

Don't park here!   Don't smoke here!   Don't hurry!   Don't worry!
No Parking.   No Smoking.   It isn't late. Everything's all right.

Pictures 1 and 2 only

1   S1   Can I park here?
    S2   No, you mustn't.
         It says 'No Parking'.

2   S1   You mustn't park here.
    S2   Why not?
    S1   Because it says 'No Parking'.

Pictures 3 and 4 only

3   S1   We needn't hurry.
    S2   Why not?
    S1   Because it isn't late.

4   S1   We don't have to hurry.
    S2   Why not?
    S1   Because it isn't late.

10

Lesson 6

Read . . .

QWERTY and Co.

Can you type? Then the chances are that you use a QWERTY keyboard. (The name comes from the top line of letters on a typewriter: QWERTYUIOP.)

5 Even the most sophisticated computer keyboard has inherited this arrangement from early typewriters. Everyone agrees that it is very inefficient: you can't type really fast on QWERTY.

You can't type really fast on QWERTY!

10 People like August Dvorak and Lillian Malt have invented far better keyboards, but few typewriter makers have the courage to drop QWERTY and make typists relearn to type!

. . . and Complete!

1 QWERTY is the order of letters which . . .
2 The arrangement on today's computer keyboards . . .

3 The main problem with QWERTY is . . .
4 Typists will have to . . . if . . .

Listen and Do!

Look at the pictures below, then take your first typing lesson!

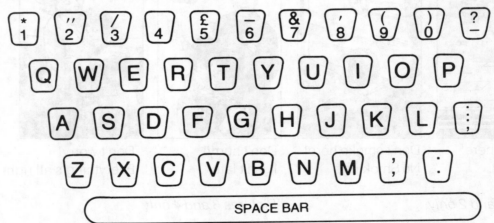

SPACE BAR

LEFT HAND

little finger	fourth finger	middle finger	forefinger

RIGHT HAND

forefinger	middle finger	fourth finger	little finger

11

A Slice of Life

Here is a picture of a modern electric typewriter.

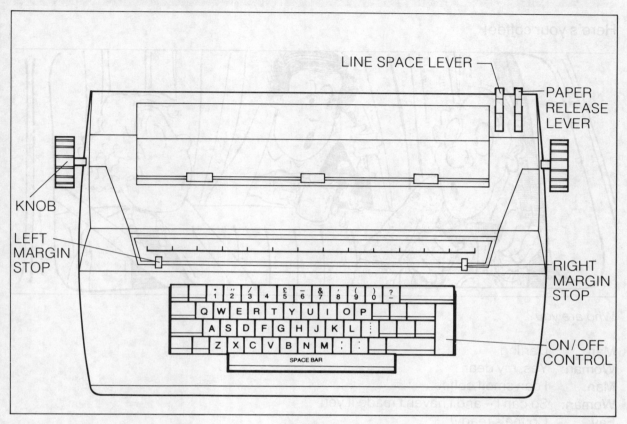

You are getting ready to type. Describe what you are doing as you do it.

Writing/Homework

Guided Summary

Read the text on page 11 again. Complete these sentences to tell us about the QWERTY keyboard. Your answer should be in one paragraph of not more than 55 words.

1   The QWERTY keyboard gets its name from . . .
2   This keyboard was used for early typewriters and is still . . .
3   Though better keyboards have been invented, . . .

Composition

Look at the picture of the typewriter in A Slice of Life above. Write a few sentences saying how you get ready to type. For example:

The first thing I do is to put in a piece of paper. To do this, I . . .

Lesson 7

Help!

Here's your coffee!

Who are you?

Man:	Darling.
Woman:	Yes, my dear.
Man:	I can smell coffee.
Woman:	So can I – and I haven't made it yet!
Fay:	Coffee's ready!
Man:	Did you hear that?
Woman:	Yes, I think someone said coffee's ready.
Man:	But you haven't made it yet! Heavens!
Narrator:	The driver stopped the Somna suddenly.
Fay:	Careful! Why did you stop so suddenly? Your coffee's . . .
Narrator:	The man and the woman turned round in amazement.
Man:	Who are you?
Woman:	Who is this woman?
Man:	I don't know my love. I have no idea.
Narrator:	There was a loud crash. Fay dropped the coffee on the man's foot.
Fay:	Help!
Narrator:	. . . she cried weakly. Then she fell, too, with a loud crash.

Talk about the Story!

1   Why is Fay so surprised?
2   Why are the man and the woman so surprised?

Study!

1 **yet**
 Yet *means 'up to this moment'. We normally use it in*
 Questions: Is the coffee ready **yet**?
 Have you made the coffee **yet**?
 Negatives: The coffee isn't ready **yet**.
 I haven't made the coffee **yet**.

2 **still**
 Still *means 'up to this moment'. We normally use it to emphasize continuity in*
 Questions: Is the coffee **still** hot? (= Does it continue to be?)
 Are you **still** making the coffee?
 Affirmatives: The coffee is **still** hot.
 I'm **still** making the coffee.

3 **already**
 Already *means 'so soon' and we normally use it in*
 Questions: Is the coffee **already** cold? (so soon)
 Have you **already** made the coffee?
 Affirmatives: The coffee is **already** cold.
 I've **already** made the coffee.

Practise!

preparing the vegetables   making the coffee   washing the dishes

UNFINISHED JOBS

1 S1 Have you made the coffee yet?
 S2 No, I haven't made it yet.
 I'm still making it.

2 S1 Are you still making the coffee?
 S2 Yes, I'm still making it.

FINISHED JOBS

3 S1 Have you made the coffee yet?
 S2 Yes, I've already made it.
 S1 That was quick!

4 S1 Have you already made the coffee?
 S2 Yes, I made it a moment ago.

Lesson 8

Grow your own fuel!

Every time we travel by boat, by car,
or by plane, we use energy. So the
need to find sources other than fossil
fuels has become very great. Plants
5 might provide the answer. We can get
gas, like methanol, from rubbish; or
liquid, like alcohol, from sugar. Most
cars in Brazil already run on 'gasohol'
(fuel containing 20% alcohol).
10 In Sweden and America, scientists are
trying to get energy from fast-growing
trees. Perhaps in future we won't dig
for fuel. We'll grow it!

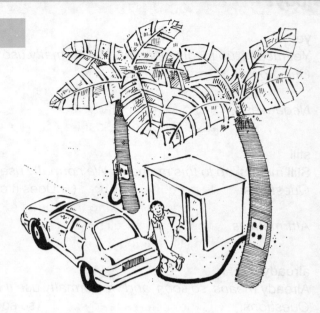

We'll grow it!

. . . and Complete!

1 Because . . . our great use of energy, we need to find different sources of fuel.
2 . . . plants can provide the answer.
3 Fuels like methanol and alcohol can be . . . from rubbish and sugar.
4 'Gasohol' . . . 20% alcohol.
5 Perhaps in the future we can grow our fuel . . . we won't have to dig for it.

Listen and Take Notes!

You are listening to a lecture on oil production.

1 *On a separate sheet of paper, complete the notes below as you listen:*

In the early seventies, the price _____

The oil producing countries _____

Countries that used a lot of oil _____

More and more countries _____

In the eighties _____

It is a strange thing _____

2 *Now, using these notes, give the lecture yourself.*

15

A Slice of Life

Here are four ways of producing power without using oil:

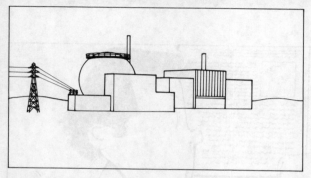

Nuclear power stations

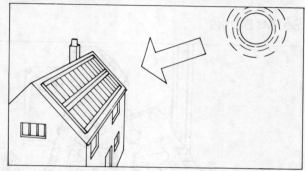

The sun: solar energy

The sea: the tides

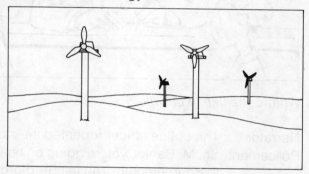

The wind: windmills

Talk about the advantages and disadvantages of the four sources of energy shown in these pictures.

Writing/Homework

Guided Summary

Read the text on page 15 again. Complete these sentences to describe the idea of growing fuel instead of digging for it. Your answer should be in one paragraph of not more than 50 words.

1 Plants can be a source ...
2 For example, alcohol can be obtained ...
3 In Brazil, 20% alcohol is added to ...
4 Another source of energy in Sweden is ...
5 Perhaps we can grow our fuel so that ...

Composition

Write two sentences on each of the forms of energy discussed in A Slice of Life.

Lesson 9

Help!

So, Mr Banks . . .

What's she like, your wife?

Narrator: The police officer repeated the story for the eleventh time.

Policeman: So, Mr Banks, you're going on holiday with your family to Bournemouth. You left Bradford early this morning and came down the motorway. Then you left the motorway and stopped to buy a paper at a little place called Stanway. It was 11 o'clock. Then you stopped about fifteen minutes later here, in Stow, and went into the back of your Somna-Mobile, but your wife wasn't there.

Bertie: That's right, officer.

Policeman: Imagine losing your wife, just like that. I can't believe it! What's she like, your wife?

Bertie: Well, she's 30 years old. She's 1 metre 70 tall. She's got brown hair and brown eyes. She's wearing a pink blouse and blue jeans.

Policeman: Perhaps she got off at Stanway.

Vicki: *We* didn't hear her. I think . . .

Narrator: Eddie began to cry.

Eddie: I want my mum.

Policeman: Don't worry, sonny. We'll find her.

Talk about the Story!

1 Why, do you think, did the police officer repeat the story for the eleventh time?
2 What new information do we learn about the characters and what they were doing?

Study!

1 *Verb +* **to-***infinitive*
When we wish to use another verb after the following, that verb can only be a **to-***infinitive:*
can afford, decide, manage, offer, prepare, want:
Affirmative: I decided to try on a jacket.
Negative: I decided not to buy it.

2 *Verb +* **-ing**
*When we wish to use another verb immediately after the following, that verb can only be
an* **-ing** *form:* **enjoy, feel like, finish, can't help, imagine:**
Affirmative: Finish eating your dinner.
Negative: Imagine not knowing the answer to such an easy question.

3 *Verb +* **to** *or* **-ing***: no change in meaning*
The following verbs can be followed by a **to-***infinitive or the* **-ing** *form without a change in
meaning:* **begin, continue, start:**
When he heard what Vicki said, Eddie **began to cry** (*or* **began crying**).

4 *Verb +* **to** *or* **-ing***: different meanings*
The **to-***infinitive or the* **-ing** *form do not mean the same after:*
remember: I remembered to post your letter. (I didn't forget to do it.)
I remember posting your letter. (I can recall doing it.)
try: You must try to pass your exam. (Make an effort to.)
Try holding your breath for a minute. (See what it's like.)
stop: Bertie has stopped to buy a newspaper. (He wanted to buy a newspaper.)
Bertie has stopped buying newspapers. (He doesn't buy them any more.)

Practise!

*Put these verbs together to make good
sentences:*

Example: Some people can't help
worrying about little things.

can afford		repeat
decide		pay
manage		buy
offer		sell
prepare		help
want		leave
enjoy		go
feel like		say
finish	+ ONE OF THESE:	eat
can't help		stand
imagine		talk
begin		work
continue		lose
start		cry
remember		wear
try		worry
stop		find

Lesson 10

Read . . .

Home sweet home?

We hardly need to go anywhere for anything. We can do so many things at home. For example, we can watch a football match on TV; we can watch a
5 film on video; we can listen to a concert on the radio or on compact disc; we can study or play games on personal computers; we can talk to our friends on the telephone. Soon

A stay-at-home society?

10 computers will enable many of us to work at home and to do our shopping from home. The question is, do we want to become a stay-at-home society?

. . . and Interpret!

1 'Home Sweet Home' is an expression which suggests that home is the best place in the world. Why is there a question-mark after it in the title?

2 Explain in a sentence what living in a stay-at-home society will be like. Tell us in a sentence why such a society would be good or bad.

Listen, Do and Explain!

You are listening to instructions about a compact disc player.

1 *Look at the pictures below and mime the movements you would have to make:*

1 RECORDING

2 PRESS

3 HOLD AT THE EDGE

4 PRESS 'OPEN'
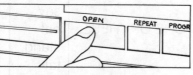

5 DRAWER SLIDES OUT

6 PLACE DISC IN DRAWER

7 DO NOT PUSH!
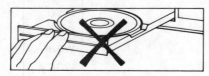

8 PRESS 'OPEN' AGAIN
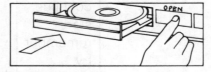

9 PRESS 'START'
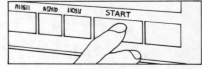

2 *Now look at the pictures and give the instructions yourself.*

19

A Slice of Life

Here are six means of home entertainment.

Talk about each one of them and say which you prefer and why.

Television

Video

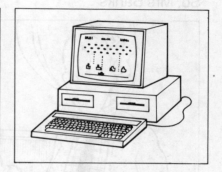

Personal computer

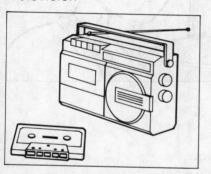

Radio/cassette player

Book

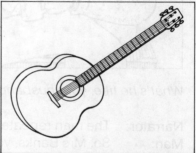

Guitar
(any musical instrument)

Writing/Homework

Guided Summary

Read the text on page 19 again. Complete these sentences to tell us about home entertainment. Your answer should be in one paragraph of not more than 70 words.

1 We can 'go to a football match' by . . .
2 We can 'go to the cinema' by . . .
3 We can 'go to a concert' by . . .
4 We can 'go to school' by . . .
5 We can 'meet our friends' by . . .
6 We can do all these things by just . . . !

Composition

Write one or two sentences on each of the means of home entertainment discussed in A Slice of Life above. Then tell us which one you prefer and why.

Lesson 11

Help!

So, Mrs Banks . . .

What's he like, your husband?

Narrator:	The man repeated Fay's story.
Man:	So, Mrs Banks, your husband stopped here in Stanway, outside the newsagent's, fifteen minutes ago and you went into the supermarket to buy some coffee. Your husband didn't know you weren't in the back of the Somna and . . .
Woman:	He must have known she wasn't there.
Man:	Quiet, Matilda. He didn't know and must have driven away. Then we stopped and our Somna is exactly the same as yours. So you got in and made coffee. Here, have another cup.
Fay:	Thanks, I need it.
Man:	What's he like, your husband?
Fay:	Well, he's 34 years old and he's 1 metre 80 tall. He's got black hair and blue eyes. We're going to Bournemouth for our holiday. I can't believe I've lost my husband and my children. It can't be true!
Man:	Don't worry, Mrs Banks. I'm sure we'll find them. They must be somewhere near here.

Talk about the Story!

1   Starting at the beginning, tell us how Fay got into this situation.
2   Are Matilda and her husband both helpful? Why/Why not?

Study!

CERTAINTY and UNCERTAINTY with modal verbs

1   *We can express certainty and uncertainty on a scale like this:*
    Present reference   *Past reference*
    You **might be** mistaken!   You **might have been** mistaken! *(very uncertain)*

    You **may be** mistaken!   You **may have been** mistaken!   *(uncertain)*

    You **must be** mistaken!   You **must have been** mistaken! *(near-certain)*

    You **are** mistaken!   You **were** mistaken!   *(certain)*

2   *We generally use* **must be** *and* **must have been** *for DEDUCTION:*
    The negative of **must be** *is* **can't be** (NOT 'mustn't be')
    The negative of **must have been** *is* **can't have been** (NOT 'mustn't have been')

    That isn't John Smith. You **must be** mistaken.
    That is John Smith. You **can't be** mistaken.

    That wasn't John Smith. You **must have been** mistaken.
    That was John Smith. You **can't have been** mistaken.

3   *We must not confuse NECESSITY (see Lesson 5) with DEDUCTION:*
    You **must leave** at once!   *(necessity)*
    You **must be** on time!   *(necessity)*
    You **mustn't smoke** here.   *(prohibition)*
    You **had to stop** at the light. *(past necessity)*

Practise!

the phone is ringing   the window is open   the door is locked

S1 makes a statement and S2 decides whether Bertie is/was in or out. For example:

Present reference:
S1 The phone is ringing.
S2 Bertie may be out./He must be out.
    He can't be in. etc.

Past reference:
S1 The phone was ringing.
S2 He may have been out./He must have
    been out. He can't have been in. etc.

Lesson 12

Lean on me!

Work on the Tower of Pisa was begun
in 1174 by the architect Bonanno. The
Tower was built on shallow foundations
and it began to lean immediately. It
5 is over 55 metres tall and is now
more than 4 metres out of true.
Meanwhile, over the centuries, people
have been suggesting ways of
preventing it from falling down. Perhaps
10 the strangest idea is to build next to it
a big bronze statue, like the Statue
of Liberty. Then the famous Tower
could lean on the statue's shoulder!

. . . could lean on the statue's shoulder!

. . . and Choose!

1 The Tower began to lean because the
foundations were
a) four metres out of true. b) not deep
enough. c) without support.

2 People have been making suggestions
over the centuries to
a) prevent the Tower from falling down.
b) build a bronze statue next to it.
c) support the tower on a statue.

Listen and Interpret!

*You are a tourist in London and a guide is
telling you about Trafalgar Square. Explain
in your own language the gist of what you
hear to a friend beside you who doesn't
know any English.*

A Slice of Life

Here is a cartoon.

1   *What point is the cartoonist making?*
2   *What are the advantages and disadvantages of living in a) a flat b) a house?*
3   *Would you prefer to live in a flat or a house? Why?*

Writing/Homework

Guided Summary

Read the text on page 23 again. Complete these sentences to tell us about the Tower of Pisa. Your answer should be in one paragraph of not more than 60 words.

1   From the moment it was begun in 1174, the Tower . . . because . . .
2   For centuries people have been afraid that . . .
3   Someone has suggested that if a big bronze statue . . .

Composition

Write a short paragraph comparing living in a flat with living in a house. Then say which you would prefer and why.

Lesson 13

Help!

Let's go different ways

Calling all cars.

Bertie:	Let's go different ways.
Policeman:	That's right, Mr Banks. You can go back to Stanway and I'll send a message to police cars in the area.
Vicki:	Do you like quizzes, officer?
Policeman:	Yes, I do.
Vicki:	Would you like to answer these questions?
Policeman:	Why don't you ask your brother?
Vicki:	He can't answer them.
Policeman:	And I can't either. Now I must find your mother. I have important work to do.
Narrator:	The message went out from Stow Police Station:
Policeman:	Calling all cars . . . calling all cars . . .
Narrator:	Meanwhile, somewhere north (or south, or east, or west) of Stow, two policemen in a radio car are talking.
Phil:	Did you understand that message, Steve?
Steve:	Not a word, Phil.
Phil:	Neither did I. We have to find a woman who fell out of a Somna or something. They're mad!

Talk about the Story!

1 What do you think is going to happen next?
2 Why do you think the policemen were puzzled by the message? Give as many reasons as you can.

Study!

AGREEING

Here are two ways we can agree with someone:

1   **Too** *and* **either** (= also)
    We use **too** *in the affirmative and* **either** *in the negative:*

Eddie: I'm thirsty.
Vicki: I am **too**.

Eddie: I'm not hungry.
Vicki: I'm not **either**.

Eddie is thirsty and Vicki is **too**.
Eddie isn't hungry and Vicki isn't **either**.

2   **So** *and* **neither**
    We can begin affirmatives with **so** *and negatives with* **neither**:

Eddie: I'm thirsty.
Vicki: **So** am I.

Eddie: I'm not hungry.
Vicki: **Neither** am I.

Eddie is thirsty and **so** is Vicki.
Eddie isn't hungry and **neither** is Vicki.

3   *When there isn't a word like* **am, is, have, has, can, will,** *etc. we use* **do, does,** *or* **did**:

Eddie: I like ice-cream.
Vicki: I **do** too. *or:* So **do** I.

Eddie: I don't like medicine.
Vicki: I **don't** either. *or:* Neither **do** I.

Eddie likes ice-cream and Vicki **does** too. *or:* . . . and so **does** Vicki.
Eddie doesn't like medicine and Vicki **doesn't** either. *or:* . . . and neither **does** Vicki.

Practise!

I'm thirsty.

I like ice cream.

thirsty	ice-cream
hungry	medicine
tired	tea
happy	coffee
bored	milk

1   *S1 makes a statement with* **I am** *or* **I'm not**
    and S2 agrees.
    S1 I'm hungry.
    S2 I am too. *or* So I am.

S1 makes a statement with **I like** *or* **I don't**
like and S2 agrees.
S1 I like ice-cream.
S2 I do too. *or* So do I.

2   *S1 and S2 talk about Eddie and Vicki.*
    S1 Eddie is hungry.
    S2 Vicki is too. *or* So is Vicki.

S1 and S2 talk about Eddie and Vicki.
S1 Eddie likes ice-cream.
S2 Vicki does too. *or* So does Vicki.

Lesson 14

Read . . .

This English!

'American' (according to an American
dictionary) is 'the English language
spoken in the US'. 'English'
(according to the same dictionary) is 'the
5 language used in Britain, the USA
and Canada'. In other words,
Americans do not usually call their
language 'American'. But, of course,
there are many Americanisms. The famous
10 US author, Mark Twain, once described

The famous US author, Mark Twain . . .

the English language as 'a joint stock
company in which the Americans own
most of the shares'.

. . . and Interpret!

1 Why does the writer say that Americans do
not usually call their language 'American'?

2 What did Mark Twain mean?

Listen and Decide!

*Listen to the text as often as is necessary to find eleven American words and the British
equivalents.*

	AMERICAN ENGLISH	BRITISH ENGLISH
1		
2		
3		
4		
5		
6		
7		
8		
9		
10		
11		

A Slice of Life

Here is a picture of 'an old banger' *(a clunker in American English).*

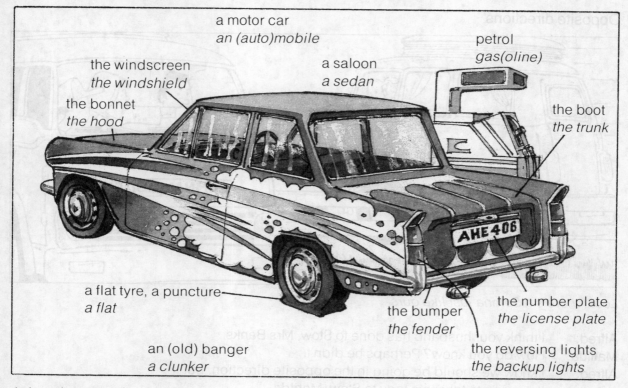

a motor car
an (auto)mobile

petrol
gas(oline)

the windscreen
the windshield

a saloon
a sedan

the bonnet
the hood

the boot
the trunk

AHE 406

a flat tyre, a puncture
a flat

the bumper
the fender

the number plate
the license plate

an (old) banger
a clunker

the reversing lights
the backup lights

Ask and answer:

1 S1 What's the English word for *a sedan*?
   S2 It's 'a saloon'?

2 S1 What's 'the bonnet' called in American English?
   S2 It's called *the hood*.

Writing/Homework

Guided Summary

Read the text on page 27 again. Complete these sentences to tell us about British and American English. Your answer should be in one paragraph of not more than 30 words.

1 The British call their language English and the Americans usually . . .
2 But there are quite a few differences . . .
3 More people speak American English than . . .

Composition

Refer to the lists of words you made in Listen and Decide! Write a very short story using some of these words. Write the same story twice: first an 'English' version, then an 'American' version.

Lesson 15

Help!

Opposite directions

Look, there's a Somna just like ours.

Alfred:	I think your husband has gone to Stow, Mrs Banks.
Matilda:	How do you know? Perhaps he didn't.
Alfred:	I know we should be going in the opposite direction, but I'm going to take this lady to Stow, Matilda.
Matilda:	Very well, Alfred.
Fay:	Thank you very much.
Narrator:	Alfred drove fast.
Matilda:	Please don't drive so fast, Alfred.
Alfred:	Yes, my love,
Narrator:	. . . said Alfred as he drove faster.
Fay:	I'm so tired. I'll have a little sleep. Please wake me up when we get to Stow.
Alfred:	Poor woman!
Matilda:	Keep your eyes on the road, Alfred!
Narrator:	A little later they saw a Somna just like theirs.
Alfred:	Look, Matilda. There's a Somna just like ours.
Vicki:	Look, Eddie. There's a Somna just like ours.

Talk about the Story!

1 Why didn't Bertie and the children try to stop the other Somna?
2 Why didn't Alfred and Matilda try to stop the other Somna? Give as many reasons as you can.

29

Study!

The verb **have**

1   *The verb* **have** *is used in three ways:*
    – *as an auxiliary verb in e.g. the Present Perfect:*
      I **have** finished work for the day.
    – *in the same way as* **have got** *to mean 'possess':*
      My neighbour **has** (*or* **has got**) a very nice car.
    – *as an ordinary verb meaning* **eat, drink,** *etc.:*
      I'm **having** a very nice meal.

2   *We often use* **have** *as an ordinary verb meaning* **take,** *etc. in the imperative*
    in OFFERS: **Have** a sandwich. **Have** some potatoes. **Have** some coffee.
    and in GOOD WISHES: **Have** a nice time! **Have** fun!

3   *We use* **have** + *noun for activities, meals, etc.:*
    I'm going to **have a bath**.
    What time did you **have breakfast**?

4   *We use* **have** + *noun in place of some verbs such as* **dance, look, rest, ride, swim.**
    Let me **have a look**.
    I'm going to **have a rest**.
    I've just **had a swim**.

Practise!

1   *S1 offers and S2 accepts or refuses.*
    S1 **Have** a sandwich.
    S2 Thanks./No thanks.

a sandwich	a slice of bread
a biscuit	a cup of coffee
an orange	a piece of cake
some tea	some potatoes
some coffee	some nuts
some fruit	some grapes

2   *S1 makes a wish and S2 returns it.*
    S1 **Have** a nice time!
    S2 Thank you. Same to you.

a nice time
a nice party
a good holiday
a lot of fun

3   S1 What are you going to do now?
    S2 I'm going to swim in the river.

4   S1 What are you going to do now?
    S2 I'm going to **have a** swim in the river.

a swim in the river
a walk in the park
a ride on my bike
a rest
a wash

Lesson 16

Read . . .

Climbers above, drivers below!

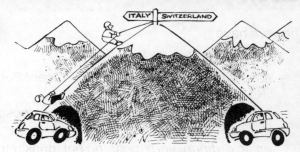

Climbers above, drivers below!

The world's longest road tunnel was opened in Switzerland on September 5th 1980. It is ten miles long and runs through the Alps, from Goschenen in
5 the Canton of Uri to Airolo in Ticino. It took 4,000 men ten years to build at a cost of 690 million Swiss francs. (The sum would be unbelievable at today's prices!) It was very expensive, but it 10 saves a lot of time and money, because traffic can now move freely in any kind of weather at the rate of 1,800 vehicles an hour. Climbers above, drivers below!

. . . and Complete!

1 This is the longest road tunnel . . .
2 It is ten miles in . . .
3 It was built at a cost of 690 million Swiss francs by . . . in . . .

4 It doesn't matter what the weather is like because . . .

Listen and Spot the Differences!

Look at the text above again. While you are reading it, listen to the recording of the listening text. See if you can spot ten differences. Make a note of them below:

TEXT ABOVE   LISTENING TEXT

1 _____   _____
2 _____   _____
3 _____   _____
4 _____   _____
5 _____   _____
6 _____   _____
7 _____   _____
8 _____   _____
9 _____   _____
10 _____   _____

A Slice of Life

There are many wonderful engineering feats in the world: bridges, dams, roads, etc.
Here are a few examples:

Brazil: The Trans-Amazon Highway.
Britain: The Flood Barriers on the Thames to prevent London from flooding.
Egypt: The Aswan Dam.
Holland: The Delta Project: a dike to keep out the North Sea in stormy weather.
Japan: The 54 km rail tunnel which joins Honshu and Hokkaido.

Here is a picture of the Flood Barriers on the Thames.

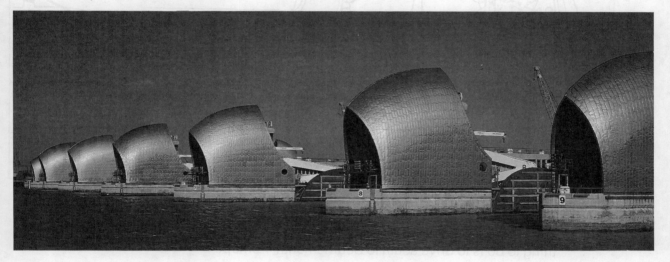

Choose a big engineering feat in this country and tell the class about it: i.e. why it was built,
how long it took to build, how much it cost, what it does, why it is such a feat and why it is
useful.

Writing/Homework

Guided Summary

Read the text on page 31 again. Complete these sentences to tell us about the world's
longest road tunnel. Your answer should be in one paragraph of not more than 50 words.

1   The longest road tunnel in the world runs ...
2   Four thousand men took ... and it cost ...
3   The tunnel allows 1,800 ...

Composition

Refer to A Slice of Life above and write one or two short paragraphs describing a famous
engineering feat in this country.

Lesson 17

Help!

South, to Bournemouth

Faster, dad, faster!

Bertie: Well, there's no sign of your mother anywhere. The only thing to do is to drive south to Bournemouth. Perhaps we'll find her there.

Eddie: Which way, dad?

Bertie: Look at the map. We're in Stanway at the moment. We can drive towards Oxford, then to Newbury and then down to Bournemouth.

Vicki: Let's go then! Why are we waiting?

Eddie: Faster, dad, faster!

Bertie: I can't go any faster. This is a Somna, not a Ferrari!

Phil: Hey, Steve. Just look at that Somna!

Steve: He thinks he's Fangio in a Ferrari!

Phil: After him, Steve!

Eddie: Dad, there's a police car behind us. Its blue light is flashing!

Bertie: Oh, dear!

Vicki: I'll ask them if they'd like to do this quiz.

Talk about the Story!

1   Do you think Bertie has made a good decision to drive to Bournemouth? Why/Why not?

2   What do you think will happen when Phil and Steve speak to Bertie?

33

Study!

1   Some, any, no *compounds*

some	any	no
someone	anyone	no one
somebody	anybody	nobody
something	anything	nothing
somewhere	anywhere	nowhere

2   *We generally use* **some** *and* **some** *compounds in affirmative statements:*
I've got **some** news for you.
I met **someone** (*or* **somebody**) who knows you well.
I bought **something** you will like.
I think he's **somewhere** in the garden.

3   *We generally use* **any** *and* **any** *compounds in:*
Questions: Have you got **any** news for me?
                    Did you buy **anything** at the market?
Negatives: I haven't got **any** news for you.
                    I didn't buy **anything** at the market.

4   *We generally use* **no** *and* **no** *compounds in place of* **not . . . any:**

I have **not** got **any** news for you.	(negative verb + **any**)
I have got **no** news for you.	(affirmative verb + **no**)
I have **not** done **anything** today.	(negative verb + **anything**)
I have done **nothing** today.	(affirmative verb + **nothing**)

Practise!

1   S1   Have you got any apples please?
       S2   No, I'm afraid we haven't got any apples today.

apples	butter
pears	cheese
bananas	yoghurt

2   S1   Have you got any apples please?
       S2   No, I'm afraid we've got no apples today.

3   S1   Is there anyone in the kitchen?
       S2   No, there isn't anyone in the kitchen.

kitchen
bedroom
bathroom
living-room

4   S1   Is there anyone in the kitchen?
       S2   No, there's no one in the kitchen.

Lesson 18

Read . . .

'We have ways of making you . . . !'

I am honest. I will not steal.

Psychologists have known for years that subliminal messages can influence people. A subliminal message can be flashed on a screen or whispered so
5 that you don't notice it *consciously*. But if it is repeated frequently, it impresses itself on your mind. In this way an advertiser on TV, for example, can make you want something. Recently
10 a supermarket in New Orleans started

broadcasting a whispered message, 'I am honest. I will not steal,' which has stopped shop-lifting in the store.

. . . and Answer!

1 What do you think a 'subliminal message' is?
2 How can a subliminal message influence human behaviour?

3 What use can TV advertisers make of subliminal messages?
4 What effect has a subliminal message had in a New Orleans supermarket?

Listen and Take Notes!

You are listening to a lecture about psychologists who try to influence the way people behave.

1 *On a separate sheet of paper, fill out the clues below as you listen:*

Some psychologists try to influence the way _____

These psychologists often work with people who _____

These people behave _____. The psychologists try to make them behave _____

This is the _____

_____ they get a prize.

For example, _____

When the same people do something 'wrong' _____

Psychologists have found that they can influence _____

2 *Now, using these notes, give the lecture yourself.*

3 *There was a subliminal message in the listening text. What was it?*

A Slice of Life

Here are the results of a survey about fears. People were asked the question:

What do you fear most?

Fear	Percentage
Speaking in front of a group	41%
Heights	32%
Insects and bugs	22%
Financial problems	22%
Deep water	22%
Sickness	19%
Death	19%
Flying	18%
Loneliness	14%
Dogs	11%
Driving/riding in a car	9%
Darkness	8%
Lifts	8%
Escalators	5%

Talk about this survey in class:
1 Do you think that some things in the list are surprising? If so, what and why?
2 What do people fear about the items in the list and why?
3 What would your choice of items be and in what order?

Writing/Homework

Guided Summary

Read the text on page 35 again. Complete these sentences to describe the effect of subliminal messages. Your answer should be in one paragraph of not more than 45 words.

1 If a message is _subliminal_ we don't . . . but it can . . .
2 TV advertisers can use messages to . . .
3 Recently, a New Orleans supermarket successfully used a subliminal message to . . .

Composition

Refer to the survey in A Slice of Life above and say which five things YOU fear most and why.

Lesson 19

Help!

South, to Bournemouth?

Here's your jar of coffee and goodbye!

Alfred: I'm afraid we can't find them here, Mrs Banks. We'll have to leave you in Stow, because we're going in the opposite direction. If you wait on the corner, I'm sure someone will give you a lift to Bournemouth.

Matilda: Here's your jar of coffee, and goodbye!

Fay: Thank you for your help. You've both been very kind.

Narrator: The Somna disappeared down the street. Fay waited on the corner holding her jar of coffee. After a while she saw a very old car approaching. It was driven by a little old lady. The little old lady stopped and spoke to Fay.

Old lady: Can I help you, my dear?

Fay: I want to go to Bournemouth. Are you going that way?

Old lady: I'm going south as far as the motorway. If you come with me, I'll leave you near the motorway.

Fay: Oh, that's very kind.

Old lady: I never drive on motorways. Everyone goes so fast. I'm getting too old for motorways and so is my little car!

Talk about the Story!

1   Do you think Fay is lucky that the old lady is going to give her a lift? Why/Why not?
2   What would you do in Fay's situation? Why?

Study!

Sentences with **if**

1   **If** *is followed by the Simple Present tense, NOT the Future:*

If + *Simple Present*
If Fay **waits** on the corner,
If Fay **is** patient,

Simple Future
someone **will give** her a lift.
she **will get** a lift.

2   **Shall** *can sometimes be used in place of* **will** *in the first persons singular and plural:*

Will you go for a swim?

Yes, I/we **shall**, if it's fine.
No, I/we **shan't**, if it isn't fine.

Except in short answers (**Yes, I shall,** *etc.):*
– **shall** *and* **will** *are shortened to* **'ll**:
   I'll go for a swim if it's fine.
– **shall not** *and* **will not** *are shortened to* **shan't** *and* **won't**:
   I shan't/won't go for a swim if it isn't fine.

Practise!

Match these sentences with the people in the picture:

If the cyclist tries to overtake me, I'll wait.
If the bus pulls out, I'll ride behind it.
If I hurry, I'll have time to cross.
If the woman tries to cross, I'll stop.

If the car behind me wants to overtake, I'll slow down.
If the car in front slows down, I'll overtake.

Look at the picture and . . .

1   *. . . make affirmative statements from the point of view of each person:*
   S   If the car stops, I'll cross the road. etc.

2   *. . . make affirmative statements from the point of view of an observer:*
   S   If driver B stops, the woman will cross the road. etc.

3   S1   Will the woman cross the road if driver B stops?
   S2   Yes, she will.
   S1   Will she cross the road if he doesn't stop?
   S2   No, she won't. etc.

Lesson 20

Read . . .

Going up?

Arthur C. Clarke, the science fiction author, has often accurately predicted the future. In 1939 he described a moon landing in detail – thirty years
5 before it happened. In 1945 he forecast world-wide communication satellites. In 1980 he predicted a lift, 22,000 miles high. One day this will be set up near the equator and attached
10 to a satellite in space. If it is built, people and equipment will be able to travel into space much more cheaply than by present-day rockets.

. . . a lift, 22,000 miles high

. . . and Choose!

1 The remarkable thing about Arthur C. Clarke's predictions is that they
a) are science fiction. b) will really happen. c) have often come true.
2 Compared with present-day rockets, a lift into space would be
a) much slower. b) much faster. c) much less expensive.

Look, Listen and Say!

The year is 1900. You are predicting what the world will be like in the year 2000. Refer to the pictures below and make three 'predictions'. Begin: 'In the year 2000 . . .'

The Jumbo Jet   TV   The motor-car

Now listen to the cassette. After you have heard it, predict 'the future' again!

A Slice of Life

Here is some information about our solar system.

PLANET	DISTANCE FROM SUN IN MILLIONS OF MILES	LENGTH OF DAY	LENGTH OF YEAR	SURFACE TEMPERATURE (Max)
MERCURY	36	59 days	88 days	400°C
VENUS	67	243 days	224.7 days	500°C
EARTH	93	23 hrs 37 min	365 days	60°C
MARS	141.5	24 hrs 56 min	687 days	21°C
JUPITER	483	9 hours	11 years	−130°C
SATURN	886	10 hours	29 years	−160°C
URANUS	1,783	10 hours	84 years	−210°C
NEPTUNE	2,793	15 hours	164 years	−230°C
PLUTO	3,666	6 days 9 hours	247 years	Not known

Ask and answer like this, e.g.:

S1 How far is Mercury from the sun?
S2 It's 36 million miles.
S1 How long is a day on Mercury?
S2 59 days.
S1 What's the length of a year on Mercury?
S2 It's 88 days etc.

Writing/Homework

Guided Summary

Read the text on page 39 again. Complete these sentences to tell us about Arthur C. Clarke's predictions. Your answer should be in one paragraph of not more than 50 words.

1 In 1939 Arthur C. Clarke, the science fiction author, predicted ...
2 In 1945 he predicted ...
3 In 1980 he predicted ...
4 One day people will use it to ...

Composition

Refer to the information in A Slice of Life. Write one or two sentences about each planet.

Lesson 21

Help!

Phil and Steve find Bertie

85 miles an hour, eh, Fangio?

Steve: 85 miles an hour, eh, Fangio?
Bertie: I'm sorry officer.
Phil: Look out, everyone! Fangio in his Somna! And now all you can say is that you're sorry.
Bertie: I'm sorry, officer. You see, I'm in a hurry.
Steve: Yes, we noticed that, didn't we Phil?
Bertie: You see, we're going on holiday to Bournemouth, but I've lost my wife and I've got to find her.
Steve: Hey, Phil. That radio message! This is our man! Your wife fell out of the Somna, didn't she?
Bertie: No, she didn't fall out. She . . .
Phil: All right. It's OK, but you shouldn't drive so fast.
Steve: Don't do it again!
Bertie: I won't, officer. I promise.
Steve: OK. We'll let you off this time, Fangio.
Vicki: I think she fell out. Do you boys do quizzes?
Eddie: Oh, shut up, Vicki!

Talk about the Story!

1 Why do you think that the two policemen let Bertie off?
2 Tell us something about the characters of Bertie, Fay, Vicki and Eddie.

Study!

Phrasal verbs

1   *We use prepositions* (**at**) *or adverb particles* (**out**) *after many common English verbs. We call these combinations phrasal verbs: e.g.* **look at, pull out.** *We often change the primary meaning of a verb when we put a preposition or a particle after it to form a new verb. phrasal verbs often (but not always) have idiomatic meanings:*

make **out** (= see):   I can just make **out** a bird in that tree.
make **up** (= invent):   My brother is good at making **up** stories.
make **for** (= go to):   After a short rest, we made **for** the nearest town.

2   *There are four types of phrasal verbs:*
    Type 1:   verb + preposition: I am looking **at** a photo.
        Type 1 verbs are followed by an object. The preposition is never separated from the verb. Other Type 1 verbs are: **believe in, listen to, look after,** *etc.*
    Type 2:   verb + adverb particle: Turn **off** the light. Turn the light **off.**
        Type 2 verbs are followed by an object. The particle CAN *be separated from the verb. The particle can be used before a noun, but not before a pronoun:*
        Turn **off** the light.   Turn the light **off.**   Turn the light **off.**
                                   Turn it **off.**   Turn them **off.**
        Other Type 2 verbs are: **pull out, put on, take off, wake somebody up,** *etc.*
    Type 3:   verb + particle: Bertie got **into** his car and drove **away.**
        Type 3 verbs are NOT *followed by an object. Other Type 3 verbs are:*
        hurry up, sit down, stand up, pull up (= stop), **turn round,** *etc.*
    Type 4:   verb + particle + preposition: We've run **out of** matches.
        Type 4 verbs are followed by an object. Other Type 4 verbs are:
        come down from, fall out of, keep out of, look up to, *etc.*

Practise!

1   *S1 asks a question and S2 answers freely.*
    S1 What are you looking at?
    S2 This photo.

look at	listen to
look for	think of
laugh at	wait for

2   *S1 makes a request and S2 echoes it.*
    S1 Turn off the light please.
    S2 Yes, turn it off please.

turn on	take off
turn off	pull out
put on	wake up

3   *S1 and S2 (or Ss) make up contexts.*
    For example, S1 goes out of the room
    and knocks at the door:
    S2: Come in!
    S1: Thank you.

come in	sit down
go away	stand up
hurry up	look up

Lesson 22

Read . . .

Don't milk the tourist!

It's an expensive business to visit
any big city as a tourist these days.
Even after paying for food and
accommodation, tourists have to dig deep
5 in their pockets for bus and train
fares, entrance to museums,
refreshments and useless souvenirs. Sending
postcards home has become very
expensive and a visit to a show can nearly
10 bankrupt you. On top of everything
else, some countries charge their
visitors a heavy airport tax when they
are leaving. Is it right to 'milk' the
tourist in this way? What do you think?

. . . and Complete!

1 When . . ., tourists have to dig deep in their
pockets for bus and train fares.
2 It is very expensive if a tourist wants . . . or
to . . .
3 Some countries make their visitors . . .
when they are leaving.

. . . *useless souvenirs*

Listen and Answer!

A friend is giving you advice about travel.

1   Listen to the advice and give oral answers to the questions below:

1 What does the speaker tell us about taxis?

2 What advice does he give about hotels?

3 How can you save yourself unnecessary
journeys to shops, banks and museums?

4 What should you know about local bus,
tram and train services? Why?

2   Refer to the questions above and give someone advice about travel.

43

A Slice of Life

Here are five typical souvenirs from London.

a guard

a mug

a shopping bag

Big Ben

a key ring

a street sign

1   *If you visited London, would you buy any of them? Why/Why not?*
2   *Tell us about the kinds of things that are sold as souvenirs in this country and what you think of them.*

Writing/Homework

Guided Summary

Read the text on page 43 again. Complete these sentences to tell us about tourism.
Your answer should be in one paragraph of not more than 70 words.

1   It's expensive to be . . .
2   After you have paid for food and accommodation, you have to pay . . .
3   It costs a lot to . . . and in some countries . . .

Composition

Write two short paragraphs about souvenirs. In the first paragraph, say what you would buy if you were travelling abroad and why. In the second paragraph, say what a tourist in this country should buy and why.

Lesson 23

Help!

So near and yet so far!

They all waved madly.

Narrator:	The old lady drove at 12 miles an hour. Her tired little car went slowly uphill and slowly downhill as Fay told her story. After some time they came to a bridge and could see the motorway below. The old lady stopped by the side of the road and they both looked down at the busy motorway. Suddenly, Fay saw something that made her jump! There it was! The family Somna!
Fay:	There they are! My husband! My children!
Narrator:	Fay waved and shouted. At that moment, Vicki was looking up at the road above and saw her mother.
Vicki:	Dad! Dad! There's our mum. She's waving at us!
Eddie:	Oh, Dad, stop! Please stop!
Bertie:	I can't. I'm not allowed to!
Narrator:	Poor Bertie had to drive on as they all waved madly.
Fay:	I'll never see them again! I'm so worried! Do you know if I can go to Bournemouth on that motorway?
Old lady:	I don't know, dear. Get out here and I'm sure you'll get a lift. Don't forget your coffee – and good luck!

Talk about the Story!

1 This is the second time they have been 'so near and yet so far'. Why couldn't they find each other last time? Why can't they this time?

2 How do you think they felt as they passed each other without being able to meet?

Study!

The form and pronunciation of the Regular Past Tense

1   The past form of regular verbs always ends in **d**. But we pronounce the past in five
    different ways, depending on the verb. We can pronounce the ending as:
    – /d/   Fay **waved** to Bertie and the children.
    – /t/   Bertie **parked** his car and went to buy a newspaper.
    – /ɪd/   Fay **shouted** but her children couldn't hear her.
    – /id/   'I'm so **worried**,' Fay said.   _Or_   /aid/:   Eddie **cried** for his mum.

2   **REMEMBER!** WE DO NOT PRONOUNCE _an extra syllable in the regular past when the_
    base form of the verb ends in a sound other than /d/ _or_ /t/:
    Fay **waved** (wave); Bertie **parked** (park); I'm **worried** (worry); Eddie **cried** (cry).
    We only pronounce an extra syllable when the base form of the verb ends with the sound
    /t/ _or_ /d/: Fay **shouted** (shout); Bertie **decided** (decide).

3   _When the base form of the verb ends with the sounds below, we pronounce the regular_
    past as /t/:
    – /p/   Bertie **stopped** to buy a paper.   (stop)
    – /k/   Bertie **parked** his car outside a newsagent's.   (park)
    – /sh/   Eddie **washed** his face.   (wash)
    – /tʃ/   Eddie **watched** his father driving.   (watch)
    – /f/   Vicki **laughed** when she heard the story.   (laugh)

Practise!

Put the past forms of the verbs below in the right columns according to their pronounciation:

wave – tie – stop – shout – cry – call – enjoy – post – visit – carry – fry – look – park – answer –
help – wait – repeat – hurry – worry – start – decide – remember – wash – try – marry – want –
drop – work – turn – finish – ask – open

/d/	/t/	/ɪd/	/id/ or /aid/

1   Practise saying the past forms of the above verbs.
2   Make up sentences about the story or about yourself using the past forms of the verbs
    above. For example:
    S When she saw her husband and children, Fay **waved** to them.
       Fay **asked** the old lady if she was going to Bournemouth. etc.

Lesson 24

Read . . .

Who's who or not who's who

There are about 20,000 people in *Who's Who in France*. The editors want to know details about each person's birth, marriage and career. Then they
5 check this information carefully, because a few (very few!) try to cheat about their age and titles. If you get in, you don't stay in for life. So VIPs become anxious when a new edition
10 appears. A recent cartoon in *Le Figaro* showed a man anxiously going through the book and saying to his wife, 'Who's who or not who's who, that is the question.'

VIPs become anxious

. . . and Interpret!

1 Find the sentence that tells us that the editors of *Who's Who in France* do not always believe the information they receive from VIPs.

2 What was the point of the recent cartoon in *Le Figaro*?

Listen and Say!

*Here is a typical **Who's Who** entry.*

MASON, Andrew Arthur, author, *b* 10 June, 1939; *s* of Thomas and Catherine Mason; *m* 1964, Janet (*née* Simpson); one *s.* one *d. Educ.* Highfield School, Manchester University (BA English, 1960). Reporter, The Guardian, 1961–63. Book reviewer, The Observer, 1964–69. Travelled for five years in North Africa and Saudi Arabia. *Publ.* Moroccan Adventure (1972); The Berbers (1978); The Heart of Arabia (1982); Across the Red Sea (1987). *Recreations:* music, conversation, travel. *Address:* 27 Bradford Av, London W3, *T.* (01) 788 8432.

1 *Read the **Who's Who** entry silently.*

2 *Listen to the cassette while reading the **Who's Who** entry silently at the same time.*

3 *Refer to the entry on the left and tell us about Andrew Mason.*

A Slice of Life

*No, this is not your form for **Who's Who in France!** It is an application form to visit Australia. Write in as much information, real or imaginary, as you can.*

Application to visit Australia
(Please Complete in BLOCK Letters)

1. FAMILY NAME	2. GIVEN NAMES	3. NAME IN ETHNIC SCRIPT (if applicable)

4. PREVIOUS NAMES

5. PARTICULARS OF BIRTH
Date ....../....../......
Day Month Year Town/Village Country

6. SEX   Male   Female

7. MARITAL STATUS

8. OCCUPATION

9. PRESENT CITIZENSHIP

10. FULL POSTAL ADDRESS

Number and Street   Suburb or Village
City or County   Post Code   Telephone Number

11. PASSPORT DETAILS
Number   Place of issue   Date of issue ....../....../....... Day Month Year   Valid until ....../....../........ Day Month Year

12. PURPOSE OF INTENDED VISIT TO AUSTRALIA
Holiday ☐   Business ☐   Visit Relatives ☐   Medical Treatment ☐

13. CONTACT ADDRESS IN AUSTRALIA (if Visiting Relatives state Name and Relationship, if Visiting for Business state Name of Business Contacts and if Visiting for Medical Treatment state Name of Doctor/Hospital)

14. LENGTH OF STAY   Days   Months

15. PROPOSED DATE OF DEPARTURE FROM THIS COUNTRY ....../....../........ Day Month Year

16(a) DETAILS OF PREVIOUS VISITS TO AUSTRALIA   16(b) DETAILS OF PREVIOUS APPLICATIONS TO ENTER AUSTRALIA FOR ANY PURPOSE

17. PARTICULARS OF FAMILY MEMBERS ACCOMPANYING (see item 'a' of attached visitor visa information)

Full Name	Relationship to Applicant	Date of Birth	Sex

Ask and answer like this, e.g.:

S1 What's your family name?	S1 Where were you born?	S1 When were you born?
S2 It's . . .	S2 In . . .	S2 In . . . etc.

Writing/Homework

Guided Summary

*Read the text on page 47 again. Complete these sentences to tell us about **Who's Who in France**. Your answer should be in one paragraph of not more than 55 words.*

1 The 20,000 people in *Who's Who in France* have to give the editors . . .
2 This information is . . . because . . .
3 VIPs become anxious when a new edition appears because . . .

Composition

Refer to the form you have completed in A Slice of Life above. Using the information you provided, write a short paragraph about yourself.

Lesson 25

Help!

Lunch

Pass me your plate!

Narrator: It was 1.20 when Bertie stopped at a cafeteria.
Eddie: What about our mum?
Bertie: We'll have to look for her in Bournemouth. What can we do?
Vicki: We should go into the cafeteria and have some lunch.
That's what we should do! I'm so hungry!
Narrator: They went to the self-service counter.
Vicki: Hamburgers and chips! With mustard! Mm!
Eddie: I'm not hungry.
Bertie: You should have something to eat, Eddie. I'm not hungry,
but I'm going to have something.
Narrator: They took their food to a table and sat down. Bertie
looked at his food and began to eat it very slowly. He
was thinking of his wife. Eddie looked at his food and
decided not to eat it at all. When he thought of his
mum, he began to cry.
Eddie: I want my mum. I can't eat this.
Vicki: Good. I'll have yours. Pass me your plate!

Talk about the Story!

1 Which member of the Banks family do you like most? Why?
2 Which member of the Banks family do you like least? Why?

Study and Practise!

Compounds of **some**, **any** _and_ **no** + _to-infinitive_
We can use a **to**-_infinitive after compounds of_ **some**, **any** _and_ **no**:
I haven't got **anywhere** to live.
I've got **nowhere** to live.
I need **someone** to help me.
I haven't got **anyone** to help me. etc.
For the use of these compounds in the affirmative and negative, see Lesson 17.

Now practise the following:

1 S Have you got
      Is there   **anything** to eat?

2 S I haven't got
      There isn't   **anything** to eat.

3 S I've got
      There's   **nothing** to eat.

4 S I've got
      Here's   **something** to eat.

eat
wear
read
do
write with
eat with

Practise!

1

I'd like something to eat, please.

What about a sandwich?

Yes, I'll have a beef sandwich, please.

With or without mustard?

With mustard please.

beef
tomato
egg

with/without
mustard
salt and pepper
salad

2

I haven't got anything to wear.

What about your blue suit?
The one with white stripes.

Yes, that's a good idea.

blue suit
grey jacket
green shirt

orange dress
yellow skirt
green blouse

with/without
white stripes
brown buttons
a wide collar

Lesson 26

Read . . .

When in Rome, do as Rome does!

No one likes to make social gaffes, so
it's very important to know other
people's customs when you are
travelling abroad. In Britain, for example,
5 you should always stand on the right
if you use an escalator. In Hungary,
you should always shake hands when you
meet people. In China, you should never
give anyone a tip. In Germany, you
10 should never give anyone wrapped flowers.
In the Arab World, you should never
express admiration for a beautiful object
– or your generous Arab host will
promptly give it to you.

. . . you should always stand on the right.

. . . and Choose!

1 It's important to know other people's
customs so that you can
a) shake hands with them. b) avoid making
a fool of yourself. c) travel abroad.

2 In which part of the world shouldn't you
give money to people for services?
a) China b) Germany c) The Arab World

Listen and Decide!

A friend is giving you advice about travelling in Britain.

1 *Listen to the advice and tick (✓) the subjects mentioned:*

The man who tried to jump the queue!

using an escalator	_____
giving presents	_____
queuing	_____
visiting someone's home	_____
smoking	_____
greeting people	_____
tipping	_____
asking personal questions	_____

2 *Look at the points you have ticked and give the advice you have just heard.*

A Slice of Life

Here is part of a booking form for a short holiday in Paris.
Fill in as much information, real or imaginary, as you can.
Note: The 'stars' (*) in the form mean 'two star hotel' or 'three star hotel'.

```
BOOKING FORM/PARIS

Date of Departure: _____     Insurance:   Yes: _____   No: _____

Date of Return: _____

                                         Names of Passengers
                                         Mr Mrs     Name & Initials
Please tick the following requirements:  or Miss
Total number      Bed & Breakfast  Half Board
of nights in Paris   **   | ***     **  | ***
4 nights
5 nights
6 nights
7 nights

Rooms required: please tick:            Person booking
                                        Name
Double + double bed | Double + twin beds  Address
Room for three (1 double bed and 1 single)
Single room         | Private bathroom     Date       Signature
```

Ask and answer like this, e.g.:

S1 Have you booked for Paris?
S2 Yes, I have.
S1 When are you leaving?
S2 On Saturday, June 8.
S1 When are you coming back?
S2 On Tuesday, June 11. etc.

Writing/Homework

Guided Summary

Read the text on page 51 again. Complete these sentences to tell us about customs in other countries. Your answer should be in one paragraph of not more than 60 words.

1 When you are in Britain, you . . .
2 Hungarians always . . .
3 When in China, never . . .
4 Don't give anyone wrapped . . .
5 If you admire something beautiful . . ., you will receive it . . .

Composition

Refer to the form you have completed in A Slice of Life above. Using the information you provided, write a letter to a friend telling him or her about your plans to have a short holiday in Paris.

Lesson 27

Help!

No lunch

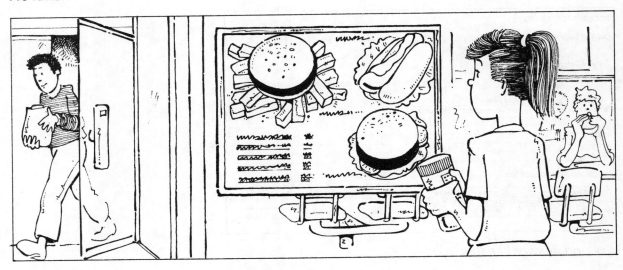

I'm so hungry!

Narrator:	After she left the old lady, Fay walked a short distance and soon arrived in a small town. It was 1.20 when she stopped outside a snack-bar.
Fay:	Mm! Hamburgers and chips! I'd love a hamburger – with mustard – and some chips! And a nice cup of tea! I'm so hungry, but I haven't got any money. I've only got this stupid jar of coffee and I can't eat that!
Narrator:	Fay was very sad, but she cheered up when she saw a young woman unlocking her car.
Fay:	Are you going to Bournemouth?
Young woman:	No, I'm going to Winchester. Will that suit you?
Fay:	Yes. Can I come with you?
Young woman:	Of course. Jump in.
Narrator:	Fay soon forgot her hunger as the young woman drove her to Winchester. In less than an hour, they were in the middle of the city.
Fay:	Thank you very much for the lift.
Young woman:	Not at all. It was a pleasure. Goodbye.

Talk about the Story!

1 Starting at the beginning, tell us how Fay has managed to get this far.
2 What do you think is going to happen next?

Study!

Requests with partitives

1   _We can make requests with_ **some**:
    I'd like **some bread** please.
    I'd like **some chips** please.
    But these requests do not tell us exactly how much bread or how many chips.
    If we want to be more exact about quantity, we have to use partitives.

2   _The most common partitive in English is_ **a piece of. A piece of** _can go with a lot of_
    uncountable nouns: e.g. **a piece of bread, a piece of chalk, a piece of paper, a piece of**
    meat, _etc. We can also use_ **a bit of: a bit of chalk,** _etc._

3   _We often use more exact partitives instead of_ **a piece of** _to go with different nouns. For_
    example:
    Singular   _Plural_
    a ball of string   3 balls of string
    a bar of chocolate/soap   4 bars of chocolate/soap
    a slice of bread/cake/meat   6 slices of bread/cake/meat

4   _Some partitives are containers:_
    a bag of flour   3 bags of flour
    a bottle of milk   4 bottles of milk
    a box of matches   2 boxes of matches
    a glass of lemonade   6 glasses of lemonade
    a packet of biscuits   6 packets of biscuits
    a cup (_or_ a pot) of tea   6 cups (2 pots) of tea
    a jar of coffee   3 jars of coffee
    a tin of sardines   2 tins of sardines
    a tube of toothpaste   2 tubes of toothpaste

Practise!

You are in a small shop and making requests for things.

1   _Singular_
    S1 Yes please (madam/sir)?
    S2 I'd like some bread please.
    S1 One loaf or two?
    S2 Just one loaf of bread please.

2   _Plural_
    S1 Can I help you (madam/sir)?
    S2 I'd like some bread please.
    S1 Will one loaf be enough?
    S2 No. Two loaves of bread please.

Lesson 28

Read . . .

View from the top

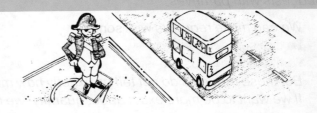

Red double-decker buses are the pride of London. If you want to get from A to B and you aren't in a hurry, it's always best to go by bus. London owes
5 its buses to George Shillibeer, who was born in 1797. He imported the idea from Paris in 1829. Within 25 years there were 500 horse-drawn buses in London and in 1856 the London General

Sit at the top of the bus!

10 Omnibus Company was formed, from which today's London Transport developed. If you want the best view of London, sit at the top of a bus!

. . . and Complete!

1 Londoners are . . . of their double-decker buses.
2 Shillibeer's date of . . . was 1797.
3 The French . . . of the idea first.

4 The London General Omnibus Company was formed and today's London Transport developed from . . .

Listen, Do and Explain!

You are listening to driving instructions about starting and moving off.

1 *Look at the pictures below, listen to the cassette and mime the movements you would have to make:*

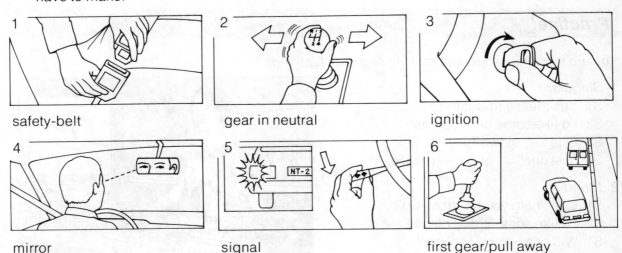

1 safety-belt	2 gear in neutral	3 ignition
4 mirror	5 signal	6 first gear/pull away

2 *Now look at the pictures and give the instructions yourself.*

55

A Slice of Life

Here is a cartoon.

1   *What point is the cartoonist making?*
2   *'Read' the pictures and tell us the story.*
3   *Discuss in class whether the story behind the cartoon is true.*

Writing/Homework

Guided Summary

Read the text on page 55 again. Complete these sentences to tell us about London buses.
Your answer should be in one paragraph of not more than 45 words.

1   London got its first buses . . .
2   The man who imported the idea from Paris was . . .
3   By 1854 there were . . . and in 1856 . . .
4   That's how today's . . .

Composition

'Read' the cartoon in A Slice of Life above and write the story.

Lesson 29

Help!

Now I can read my newspaper

Hey, dad, listen to this!

Vicki:	I enjoyed that.
Eddie:	I didn't.
Bertie:	At last! Now I can read my newspaper. I'd like to have a look at the sports page.
Narrator:	Bertie read the back page and Vicki read the front page.
Vicki:	Hey, dad, listen to this! 'TWO CHILDREN KIDNAPPED. Police are looking for a man in the Bournemouth area. The man, driving a Somna, has kidnapped two children. He is about 34 years old and about 1 metre 80 tall. He's got black hair and blue eyes. The children are a girl aged 9 and a boy aged 6.' That's bad news! Dad, are you listening?
Bertie:	No. Listen to this. 'TENNIS AT WIMBLEDON. MacDonald P. Mooseburger, U.S.A., beat Rod Digger, Australia, 6-4, 8-9, 6-2.' Imagine that!
Eddie:	I want my mum!
Narrator:	. . . Eddie shouted and he began to cry. At the next table, a man and a woman were looking at Bertie and the children very carefully. The man was writing some information on a piece of paper.

Talk about the Story!

1   Has Vicki any reason to be worried? Why/Why not?
2   What's going to happen to them next, do you think?

Study!

Nouns which are always uncountable

1 *Some nouns which can be used in the singular and plural in other languages are usually uncountable in English. This means they are not normally used with a or an and do not have a plural. For example:*

I'd like some information please.   (**information** *has no plural*)
Have you got any baggage with you?   *(We cannot have* **a** *in front of* **baggage**)
This news is interesting.   (**news** *is singular and is followed by* **is**)

2 *Here is a selection of common nouns of this kind:*
accommodation, advice, baggage, bread, business, clothing, damage, furniture, hair, homework, housework, information, lightning, luggage, macaroni, machinery, money, news, nonsense, rubbish, shopping, spaghetti, soap, thunder, toast, work.

Fruit *is normally uncountable:*   I'd like some fruit please.
Fruits *refers to varieties:*   Tropical fruits are delicious.

Practise!

1 S1 I'd like some accommodation please.
   S2 Certainly. What sort of accommodation exactly?

| accommodation |
| advice |
| information |

2 S1 How much baggage have you got?
   S2 Not much.

| baggage |
| bread |
| furniture |
| homework |
| information |
| macaroni |

3 S My hair is very long.

hair	– long
spaghetti	– cold
baggage	– heavy
work	– hard
accommodation	– cheap

4 S There's a lot of news in the paper.

| news in the paper |
| rubbish in the street |
| nonsense on TV |
| fruit in the basket |
| money in my pocket |

Lesson 30

Read . . .

Captain Morgan's treasure

Where can you find the treasure of the
pirate, Captain Henry Morgan? His ship,
the *Oxford*, sank off the coast of Haiti
on January 2, 1669. Nearly 250 sailors
5 were drowned and the ship went to the
bottom with a huge amount of pirate
treasure. Captain Morgan left a message:
'Find the narrow headland with the lonely
tree and face the shore. Walk, then swim
10 100 yards out and dive to a depth of 20
feet . . .' Which headland? Which tree? Ah,

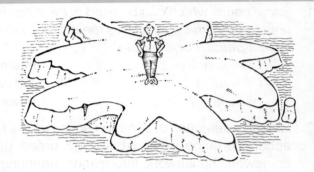

Find the narrow headland . . .

that's the secret of the French team of
divers that has just found the treasure!

. . . and Answer!

1 Who was Captain Henry Morgan?
2 What happened to his ship, the *Oxford*?
3 Why was this such a sad event?

4 What was the ship carrying?
5 What's the matter with the instructions
('Find the . . .')?

Listen and Take Notes!

You are listening to another true story about finding treasure under the sea.

1   *On a separate sheet of paper, fill out the clues below as you listen:*
1 For 17 years, the treasure-hunter, Mel Fisher _____
2 All this time _____ *Nuestra Senora de Atocha,*
   which _____ in 1622.
3 But in July, 1985 _____
4 Thousands of bars _____
5 In the first two days _____
6 Then they found _____
7 The treasure may be worth _____
8 Mel and his team _____
9 The search cost _____ and sometimes _____
10 Now _____
11 Mel, his wife Taffi and two sons, Kane and Kim, _____
12 Each member of the crew _____

2   *Now, using these notes, tell us the story.*

A Slice of Life

Here are the results of a survey on the subject:

TIME IS MONEY: HOW LONG IT TAKES TO EARN THE CASH TO BUY . . .							
The cost of living in Europe's capitals measured in hrs & mins	Bread (1 kg)	Man's suit	Washing machine	Car	Taxi journey (3 km)	Annual TV licence	Restaurant meal
In London	10 mins	39.53	312.54	1,114.15	34 mins	5.54	1.41
In Bonn	15	28.17	173.24	761.40	35	12.00	1.08
In Paris	13	61.31	283.23	1,317.56	42	10.52	1.34
In Rome	16	50.19	315.06	1,446.17	31	11.30	1.50
In Amsterdam	10	32.11	166.32	934.47	34	10.26	1.16
In Brussels	09	36.43	201.55	783.53	41	10.47	1.18
In Luxembourg	08	32.53	158.46	706.04	36	—	.57
In Copenhagen	13	28.22	165.29	1,070.10	34	12.44	1.08

Talk about the cost of living survey in class:

IS IT TRUE ONE OF OUR CLEANERS HAS INHERITED A FORTUNE?

1 How do prices compare between these European capitals?
2 How do these prices compare with the prices where you live?
3 How has the cost of living gone up in this country in the past two years?

Writing/Homework

Guided Summary

Read the text on page 59 again. Complete these sentences to tell us about Captain Morgan's treasure. Your answer should be in one paragraph of not more than 45 words.

1 Captain Morgan's ship, the _Oxford_, . . .
2 It was carrying . . .

3 French divers have interpreted some instructions and have just . . .

Composition

Refer to the survey in A Slice of Life above and write one sentence about each of the European capitals in the list.

Lesson 31

Help!

Fay arrives in Winchester

Fay followed the tourists.

Fay: I'm sure Bertie and the children won't arrive in Bournemouth till this evening. I've got plenty of time. I think I'll visit Winchester Cathedral again.

Narrator: Fay loved Winchester Cathedral and knew it very well. She was soon standing outside the great building and looking up at it in admiration. Just then, a coach parked outside the cathedral and 35 American tourists got out of it. 'You can do what you like till 3.30,' their driver said. Fay followed the tourists as they walked towards the cathedral.

Elmer: What does the guide-book say about Winchester, Edith?

Edith: Well, it says here, Elmer, that Winchester is a very important place. It used to be the capital of England, so it was more important than London.

Elmer: Really! And what does the guide-book say about Winchester Cathedral?

Edith: This cathedral was built in the 11th century.

Elmer: Just before our time, Edith!

Talk about the Story!

1 What do you think is going to happen to Fay now?
2 Do you think Fay is still as worried about her family as she was this morning? Why/Why not?

Prepositions of time

1   at, on *and* in
    REMEMBER!   **at** + *time:*   I'll see you **at** 4 o'clock.
                    on + *day:*   I'll see you **on** Monday.
                         + *date:*   I'll see you **on** March 21st.
                    in + *month:*   I'll see you **in** July.
                         + *season:*   I'll see you **in** the spring.
                         + *year:*   I'll see you **in** 1999.

2   **By** *and* **not until** (*or* **not till**)
    We use **by** *in the affirmative to mean 'any time up to':*
    We'll arrive **by** 6 o'clock.
    I should finish this work **by** Monday.
    We'll be ready for a holiday **by** July.
    We form the negative of statements like those above with **not until** (*or* **not till**):
    We **won't** arrive **until** (*or* till) 6 o'clock.
    I **won't** finish this work **until** (*or* till) Monday.
    We **won't** be ready for a holiday **until** (*or* till) July.

3   **Until** *and* **till** *in affirmative statements*
    We can use **until** *and* **till** *in the affirmative with verbs that tell us* HOW LONG *something happens:*
    We worked **until** (*or* till) 6. (That's when we stopped working.)
    We slept **until** (*or* till) 6. (That's when we woke up.)

1   S1 When do you take off for Vienna?
    S2 On Monday at 9.50.
    S1 And when do you arrive?
    S2 At 11.50.
    or We should arrive by 11.50.
    or Not until (*or* till) 11.50.

DAY .	TAKE OFF	FLY TO	LAND
Mon.	09.50	Vienna	11.50
Tue.	10.00	Brussels	11.00
Wed.	15.00	Paris	16.00

2   S1 What time will you arrive in Vienna?
    S2 We won't arrive until (*or* till) 11.50.

3   S1 How long did you work this
        afternoon?
    S2 We worked until (*or* till) 6.

| work |
| sleep |
| drive |
| play football |
| wait for Tim |
| watch TV |

Lesson 32

Read . . .

Electronic mail

How soon will your message be
delivered? We face this question every
time we post a letter. But ordinary
postal services are slow. Telex systems
5 are much quicker. You type your message
in one place and it is printed in
another – sometimes thousands of miles
away. More advanced electronic mail
services allow you to send a text or a
10 picture instantly across the world.
Your message appears at the other end
on a screen or in print – delivered by
an 'intelligent' typewriter.

Your message appears at the other end.

. . . and Interpret!

1 What is the main disadvantage of ordinary
postal services?
2 What is the difference between 'telex
systems' and 'more advanced electronic
systems'?

3 In one sentence, say how some people
benefit from electronic mail.

Look, Listen and Say!

You are going to hear a talk about sending electronic messages.

1 *Look at the pictures below and listen:*

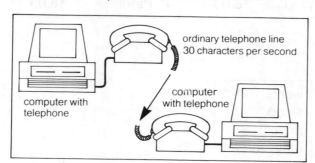

ordinary telephone line
30 characters per second

computer with
telephone

computer
with telephone

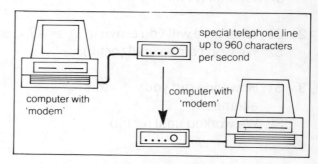

special telephone line
up to 960 characters
per second

computer with
'modem'

computer with
'modem'

2 *Look at the pictures and describe the two ways we can send information through
computers.*

A Slice of Life

Here is part of a Post Office leaflet for the public:

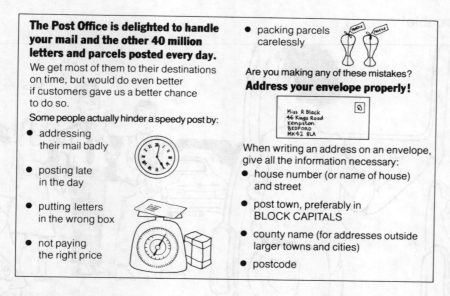

The Post Office is delighted to handle your mail and the other 40 million letters and parcels posted every day.

We get most of them to their destinations on time, but would do even better if customers gave us a better chance to do so.

Some people actually hinder a speedy post by:

- addressing their mail badly
- posting late in the day
- putting letters in the wrong box
- not paying the right price
- packing parcels carelessly

Are you making any of these mistakes?

Address your envelope properly!

Miss R Black
46 Kings Road
Kempston
BEDFORD
MK42 8LA

When writing an address on an envelope, give all the information necessary:

- house number (or name of house) and street
- post town, preferably in BLOCK CAPITALS
- county name (for addresses outside larger towns and cities)
- postcode

Talk about the Post Office leaflet:

1   Tell us about the five ways people 'actually hinder a speedy post'. How exactly do they hinder it?

2   Tell us about the leaflet. Is it attractively laid out? Is the information useful? Does this sort of leaflet help the public? Why/Why not?

3   Tell us about the postal services in this country and describe any experiences you have had with letters or parcels.

Writing/Homework

Guided Summary

Read the text on page 63 again. Complete these sentences to tell us about mail services. Your answer should be in one paragraph of not more than 40 words.

1   Telex systems are much quicker . . .
2   A message typed in . . .
3   With electronic mail you can send . . .

Composition

Write two paragraphs for a foreign friend telling him or her about postal services in this country: e.g. when and where to post letters, how quickly they are delivered, how much it costs, how envelopes are usually addressed, etc.

Lesson 33

Help!

Here comes trouble!

That's him. The kidnapper!

Narrator:	The man and the woman followed Bertie and the children out of the cafeteria and into the motorway carpark. When Bertie stopped in front of his Somna, the woman ran off to find a policeman. She returned a few moments later.
Woman:	That's him. The kidnapper!
Man:	Yes, officer. Look at this newspaper. He looks like the man in this picture and he's got a Somna.
Policeman:	Mm. This looks suspicious.
Vicki:	Look out, dad. Here comes trouble!
Policeman:	Is this your Somna, sir?
Bertie:	Yes, officer.
Narrator:	The police officer spoke into his two-way radio.
Policeman:	Officer 724 speaking. Please send a police car immediately to Motorway Cafeteria Number 14.
Eddie:	I want my mum!
Policeman:	Don't worry, sonny. Now, Mr um . . . I'd like to ask you a few questions.

Talk about the Story!

1 What do you think is going to happen to Bertie now?
2 Do the children help him, or do they make things worse for him? Why?

Study!

'Sense verbs'

1 *'Sense verbs' describe appearance, the senses or feelings. Common verbs of this kind are:* **feel, look, seem, smell, sound** *and* **taste**. *We often use these verbs in place of* **be** *when, for example, we are not sure of the facts.*

2 *'Sense verb' + adjective*
   'Sense verbs' are often followed by adjectives:

   I feel ill.   This egg tastes bad.
   You look happy.   This egg smells awful.
   She seems tired.   That music sounds terrible.

   We use adjectives, not adverbs, after 'sense verbs'. Compare:

   You look well.   = in good health: **well** *is an adjective and refers to* **you**.
   You played well.   = that's how you played: **well** *is an adverb and refers to* **played**.
   You look bad.   = not well: **bad** *is an adjective.*
   You played badly.   = **badly** *is an adverb.*

3 *'Sense verb' +* **like**
   'Sense verbs' are often followed by **like** *+ noun:*
   You look like a boxer.
   This tastes like butter.
   This looks like sugar.

Practise!

1 S1 What's the matter with him?
   S2 I'm not sure. He looks tired

feel		tired
look		hungry
seem	+	thirsty
sound		ill
		angry
		bored
		annoyed

2 S1 What *is* that?
   S2 I'm not sure. It looks like a pear

a pear	sugar
an apple	mustard
an orange	pepper

3 S1 You look good!
   S2 I feel good!

good
well
bad
ill

Lesson 34

Read . . .

Grr!

You can learn a lot about people from the way they drive. Even a mild person can become very aggressive behind the wheel of a car. Psychologists explain
5 this in many ways. Driving is very competitive. People inside vehicles are cut off from each other, so they can ignore ordinary social rules of behaviour. They push, shout and make rude
10 gestures because their bad behaviour is not punished. So if you want to find out what your future partner can *really* be like sometimes, ask him or her to take you for a drive!

Bad behaviour is not punished.

. . . and Choose!

1 Driving can affect the behaviour of
   a) every person. b) mild people only.
   c) aggressive people only.

2 The real reason why drivers behave badly is that
   a) even a mild person can become aggressive. b) they push, shout and make rude gestures. c) they know they won't be punished.

Look, Listen and Say!

Tell us about some of the things that annoy drivers.

Now listen to the cassette. After you have heard it, tell us again about some of the things that annoy drivers.

A Slice of Life

Here are THE TEN RULES OF MOTORING *from the Police Drivers' Manual.*

---

1 Perfect your Roadcraft
 - Use your skill to keep out of trouble.

2 Drive with deliberation and overtake as quickly as possible.
 - When safe, go!

3 Develop car sense and know the capabilities of your vehicle.
 - Driver and vehicle must blend to ensure skilful driving.

4 Give proper signals, use the horn and headlights thoughtfully.
 - Give good signals in good time.

5 Concentrate all the time to avoid accidents.
 - Concentration helps observation.

6 Think before acting.
 - Think and avoid accidents.

7 Exercise restraint and hold back when necessary.
 - When in doubt, wait.

8 Corner with safety.
 - Lose your speed or lose the car.

9 Use speed intelligently and drive fast only in the right places.
 - Any fool can drive fast enough to be dangerous.

10 Know the Highway Code and put it into practice.
 - Drive according to the Highway Code and you will drive safely.

Talk about THE TEN RULES OF MOTORING:

1 Tell us what you understand by each rule and give examples if you can.
2 Tell us what you think driving is like in this country. Do drivers keep to these rules? Why/Why not?

Writing/Homework

Guided Summary

Read the text on page 67 again. Complete these sentences to tell us about driving. Your answer should be in one paragraph of not more than 40 words.

1 People often behave badly behind the wheel of a car because . . .
2 As they are cut off from each other . . . without . . .

Composition

Write two paragraphs for a foreign friend giving him or her advice about driving in this country.

68

Lesson 35

Help!

Fay earns some money

Perhaps I can help you.

Elmer: William who?

Edith: It says here 'William Rufus'.

Elmer: Yes, but who *was* William Rufus?

Fay: Perhaps I can help you. England was invaded by William the Conqueror in 1066. William Rufus was his son. When his father died, William Rufus became William II, King of England. He was king from 1087 to 1100. When he died, he was buried here, in this cathedral. Winchester used to be an important place. It used to be the capital of England. It used to have a Norman castle. The castle was begun by William the Conqueror in 1066.

Narrator: The tourists stood round Fay and listened.

Edith: Now that's really interesting.

Narrator: When they left, the tourists pressed money into Fay's hand.

Fay: But please. I don't expect . . .

Elmer: You're a wonderful guide, ma'am. You're much better than Edith's guide-book.

Talk about the Story!

1 Tell us some ways you think Fay might be able to use this money.
2 What do you think Fay will do next? Why?

Study!

The Passive

1 *We form the Passive with* **be** *+ the Past Participle of a verb. The Past Participle is the* **third** *part of the verb:*

invade – invaded – **invaded** (regular verb):   England **was invaded** in 1066.
begin – began – **begun** (irregular verb):   The castle **was begun** in 1066.

Some active and passive forms are:

	Active		*Passive*	
Present Progressive:	He is writing	→	It is being	written
Simple Present:	He writes	→	It is	written
Past Progressive:	He was writing	→	It was being	written
Simple Past:	He wrote	→	It was	written
Present Perfect:	He has written	→	It has been	written
Future:	He will write	→	It will be	written

2 *We can follow a Passive verb with* **by** *+ agent. The agent is WHO or WHAT did something:*

The window was broken **by the boy**.   (The boy broke the window.)
The window was broken **by a stone**.   (A stone broke the window.)

We DO NOT USE **by** *+ agent when we do not know who did something:*

My car **was damaged** in the car park.

We ONLY USE **by** *+ agent when we wish to give important information:*

This old bridge **was built by Telford**.

3 *We often use* **by** *+ agent after verbs like* **build, compose, damage, design, discover, invade, invent, make, write,** *etc.*

England **was invaded by William the Conqueror**.

Practise!

England – invaded
William the Conqueror 1066

America – discovered
Columbus 1492

Pompeii – destroyed
a volcano AD 79

1 S1 Who **was** England invaded by?
   S2 William the Conqueror.

2 S1 When **was** England invaded?
   S2 In 1066.

3 S1 England **was** invaded by William the Conqueror.
   S2 When?
   S1 In 1066.

4 S1 England **was** invaded in 1066
   S2 Who by?
   S1 William the Conqueror.

Lesson 36

Read . . .

Winchester

Winchester is in the south of England.
It is a beautiful city with a
population of about 32,000. If you go there
you can visit the famous cathedral.
5 When the Normans invaded England in
1066, Winchester was more important
than London. It was the capital of
England until 1278. Winchester
Cathedral began as a small church in 648
10 and, over the centuries, grew to be
one of the greatest cathedrals in the
world. Quite near it, you can see the
statue of King Alfred the Great (849–
899), the city's most famous son.

When the Normans invaded England . . .

. . . and Answer!

1 How many people live in Winchester?
2 How do we know that Winchester existed
   before the Normans invaded England in
   1066?
3 How long after the Norman invasion was
   Winchester the capital of England?

Listen and Interpret!

*You are a tourist in Winchester and a guide is telling you about the place. Explain in your own
language the gist of what you hear to a friend beside you who doesn't know any English.*

A Slice of Life

Here is a map of Winchester:

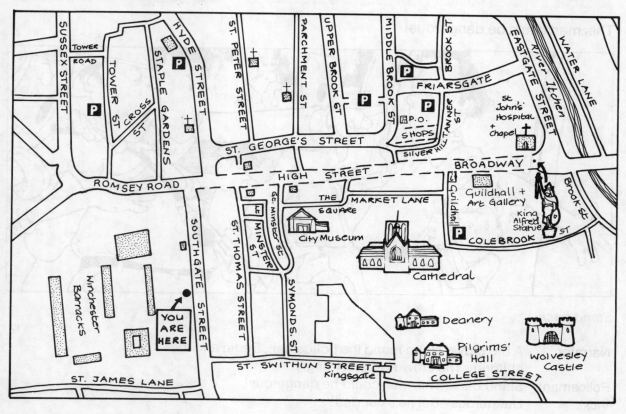

Refer to the map and ask for and give directions like this:

S1 How can I get to the High Street from here?
S2 Go straight up this street then it's first right.

Writing/Homework

Guided Summary

Read the text on page 71 again. Complete these sentences to tell us about Winchester. Your answer should be in one paragraph of not more than 45 words.

1 The city of Winchester in the south of England used to be . . .
2 It remained the capital till . . .
3 Two of the famous sights you can see there are . . .

Composition

Write two paragraphs for a foreign friend telling him or her about a town you know well in this country.

Lesson 37

Help!

This man could be dangerous!

Stand back!

Narrator:	A big crowd stood round the policeman, Bertie and the children. The crowd was very angry.
Policeman:	Stand back! This man could be dangerous!
Vicki:	Dangerous? But he's our dad!
Narrator:	. . . Vicki shouted, but, with all the noise, no one could hear a word she said.
Woman:	He looks dangerous! A dangerous kidnapper!
Man:	Yes. Look at that poor boy! He's crying!
Vicki:	Shut up, Eddie! Don't cry. You make things worse for dad!
Narrator:	But Eddie couldn't stop! At last the police car arrived and two policemen jumped out. The crowd stood back to let them through. They ran towards Bertie, the kidnapper, and then stopped suddenly.
Steve:	Heavens! It's Fangio!
Phil:	Fangio and his Somna-Ferrari. The fastest thing on four wheels!
Steve:	Ten miles an hour in sixty seconds!
Narrator:	Vicki and Bertie laughed and Eddie stopped crying.

Talk about the Story!

1   What will Phil and Steve tell the angry crowd?
2   Tell us about Bertie's earlier experience with these two policemen.

Study!

Two common ways we use can *and* could

1 *ABILITY*
   We use can *or* am/is/are able to *to express ABILITY in the present:*
   Vicki can do (*or* is able to do) a quiz in a few minutes.
   We use could (*or* was/were able to) *to express GENERAL ABILITY in the past:*
   I could swim (was able to swim) very well when I was a boy.
   If we want to refer to a **particular** *achievement, we must use* was/were able to:
   He's getting better. Yesterday he was able to have a little soup. (NOT 'could')
   But we can use could *with 'sense verbs' like* hear, see, smell, *etc.:*
   There was so much noise, no one could hear (*or* was able to hear) Vicki.
   We cannot use can *to express ABILITY in the future. We must use* will be able to:
   Our baby will be able to walk in about a month's time.

2 *POSSIBILITY and PERMISSION*
   We often use can *and* could *to say or ask whether something is possible or is allowed.* **Can**
   and **could** *are exactly the same, but* **could** *is a little more polite. We can use them to refer
   to the present:*
   Can
   Could   I speak to the manager please?
   or to refer to the future:
   Can
   Could   I see the dentist tomorrow morning please?

Practise!

stand up

walk two steps

reach the table

The present
1 S1 Look! Our baby can already stand up!
   S2 Yes! Isn't he clever! He's already able to stand up!

The past (general ability only)
2 S1 Our baby could stand up when he was only 10 months old!
   S2 Yes! Wasn't he clever! He was able to stand up when he was only 10 months old!

The future
3 S1 Our baby will be able to stand up soon!
   S2 Yes! What will he be able to do next, I wonder!

Lesson 38

Read . . .

Marketing

What is marketing? Some people think it means selling; others think it is another word for advertising. It is neither of these. It is the business

5 of creating customers by looking at what you provide (goods and services) through the eyes of the consumer. Then you can give people what they *really* want at a price they can afford

. . . *give people what they really want.*

10 to pay. This is quite different from simply making things and then trying to persuade people to buy them. In today's fast-moving business world, marketing is survival.

. . . *and Interpret!*

1 How do we know that the writer thinks many people have the wrong idea about marketing?

2 It's not enough to give people what they really want. What else is necessary?

3 Say in a sentence what you understand by the last sentence in the text.

Listen, Choose and Say!

You are going to hear a talk about the marketing of a famous product you know well.

1 *Choose the right information below:*

What did the American poet, Emerson, say?
 a) People will always buy a better mousetrap.
 b) We must make better mousetraps.

The Japanese company, Sony,
 a) introduced the Beta video system.
 b) introduced the VHS video system.

The company that introduced VHS was called
 a) 'VHS'.
 b) 'JVC'.

In the end, it was
 a) the Sony system that succeeded.
 b) the JVC system that succeeded.

What the public really wants is
 a) the cheapest system.
 b) a standard system.

2 *Now refer to the choices you have made and give us the substance of the talk you have just heard.*

A Slice of Life

Here is some advice to advertising copywriters from David Ogilvy's **Confessions of an Advertising Man**.

The two most powerful words you can use in a headline are ** FREE **
and ** NEW ** . You can seldom use FREE, but you can almost always use
NEW - if you try hard enough.

Other words and phrases which work wonders are:

** HOW TO ** SUDDENLY ** NOW **
** ANNOUNCING ** INTRODUCING **
** IT'S HERE ** JUST ARRIVED **
** IMPORTANT DEVELOPMENT **
** IMPROVEMENT ** AMAZING**
** SENSATIONAL ** REMARKABLE **
** REVOLUTIONARY ** STARTLING **
** MIRACLE ** MAGIC ** OFFER **
** QUICK ** EASY ** WANTED **
** CHALLENGE ** ADVICE TO **
** THE TRUTH ABOUT ** COMPARE **
** BARGAIN ** HURRY ** LAST CHANCE **

Look at the information above and talk about the words used in advertising.

1   Tell us what effect words like these can produce and why they might make someone want
    to buy something.
2   Tell us about advertising in this country (e.g. on TV, in the press, etc.) and your views on it.

Writing/Homework

Guided Summary

*Read the text on page 75 again. Complete these sentences to tell us about marketing. Your
answer should be in one paragraph of not more than 50 words.*

1   'Marketing' is not . . .
2   The way to create customers is to . . .
3   People will buy . . .

Composition

*Refer to A Slice of Life above and write three short pieces of advertising copy to advertise
a) a car b) soap c) a new soft-drink.*

Lesson 39

Fay spends her money

The lady at table Number 5 . . .

Elmer:	Just one more photo. Thank you.
Narrator:	Elmer took another photo of Fay and Edith. Then Fay said thank you to the friendly tourists as they got on the coach. When they had gone, Fay counted her money.
Fay:	£8.35 in tips and $2! I'm rich!
Narrator:	Suddenly, she remembered how hungry she was.
Fay:	I've got enough for a meal!
Narrator:	She looked at her watch. It was almost four o'clock, too late for lunch, but just in time for tea. Fay walked into the town centre and looked for the best teashop in Winchester. Half an hour later, the two waitresses in the teashop couldn't believe their eyes.
1st waitress:	The lady at table Number 5 came here about half an hour ago. She has just ordered more toast and more cakes. She's been eating for twenty minutes!
2nd waitress:	She's already eaten three slices of toast, a plate of sandwiches and a plate of cakes!
1st waitress:	And she's had two pots of tea!

Talk about the Story!

1   Do you think Fay has spent her money in the best way? Why/Why not?
2   Do you think Fay will find Bertie and the children before they get to Bournemouth? Why/Why not?

Study!

1 *The Present Perfect Progressive (or 'Continuous')*

I, You, We, They   have been eating . . .

He, She, It   has been eating . . .

This tense describes actions which have been in progress in the past and may or may not still be in progress. The statement:

I have been painting this room.

may mean: . . . and I'm going to continue immediately.

        or: . . . and I have stopped for the time being.

In any case, the job is not finished.

Compare the simple Present Perfect:

I have painted this room.

which means I have definitely finished the job.

2 Since *and* for

We often use the Present Perfect Progressive with:

since   +   *exact time reference*:   I have been waiting here since 6 o'clock.

for   +   *period of time*:   I have been waiting here for fifteen minutes.

3 Ago

Ago *is used with the Past Tense in phrases like* **two minutes ago, three hours ago, ten days ago, four months ago, five years ago,** *etc. Note its position at the end of the phrase:*

I had my breakfast half an hour ago.

I met him in Paris ten years ago.

Practise!

1 *You have just returned home and are talking to a member of the family. Make up conversations like this:*

S1 What have you been doing while I was out?

S2 I've been writing letters

S1 How long have you been doing that?

S2 For about two hours . *or:* Since 12 o'clock

2 *You are making suggestions to a bored child. Make up conversations like this:*

S1 Why don't you do your homework ?

S2 Because I've already done it .

S1 When did you do it ?

S2 About two hours ago .

Lesson 40

Read . . .

Profitable picnics

People have been looking for gold in
Australia since the great gold-rush
days of the 1850's. These days,
prospectors use electronic detectors. With
5 the help of one of these, three school-
boys recently found a 2½ kilo nugget.
So far, the biggest nugget has been
found by a couple in the hills north
of Melbourne. They discovered a 30 kilo
10 nugget under a few inches of soil.

They discovered a 30 kilo nugget.

Because of its shape, the nugget was
called 'The Hand of Faith'. Picnics
in the hills can be fun – and
profitable, too!

. . . and Complete!

1 These days, electronic detectors . . .
2 Recently, with the help of one of these, a
   2½ kilo nugget . . .
3 So far, a couple in Melbourne . . .

4 The 30 kilo nugget . . .
5 Picnics in the hills can not only be . . . but
   . . . too!

Listen and Spot the Differences!

*Look at the text above again. While you are reading it, listen to the recording of the listening
text. See if you can spot ten differences. Make a note of them below:*

TEXT ABOVE   LISTENING TEXT

1 _____   _____

2 _____   _____

3 _____   _____

4 _____   _____

5 _____   _____

6 _____   _____

7 _____   _____

8 _____   _____

9 _____   _____

10 _____   _____

A Slice of Life

Here are SIX AMAZING FACTS *about* GOLD!

* King Croesus of Lydia (western Anatolia in Turkey)
  struck the first pure gold coins 2,500 years ago.

* There are at least 10,000 million tons of it in the
  oceans of the world – but we still don't know how to
  get it out cheaply.

* Gold does not rust or spoil, no matter how long it
  remains in the ground.

* One ounce of gold (28.35 g) can make an unbroken
  wire 35 miles long (56.3 kms).

* The largest pure gold nugget ever found was 2 feet
  long and 1 foot across. It weighed 150 pounds (68
  kg) and was discovered in 1869 near Moliagul in
  Victoria, Australia. It was called 'Welcome
  Stranger' and was sold for £9,532.

* The largest solid gold object in existence is the
  coffin of the Egyptian king, Tutankhamun, which
  weighs 2,450 pounds. (1,111.3 kg)

LUCKY STRIKE *The largest ever gold-bearing
nugget was found in 1872 at a mine in New South
Wales (Australia). It yielded 187 pounds (84.8 kg) of
pure gold.*

Talk about this question in class:

Do you think gold is still a measure of value today? Why/Why not?

Writing/Homework

Guided Summary

*Read the text on page 79 again. Complete these sentences to tell us about profitable picnics.
Your answer should be in one paragraph of not more than 60 words.*

1 People in Australia haven't stopped looking . . . but these days they . . .
2 A nugget weighing 2½ kilos was recently . . .
3 The biggest nugget discovered so far weighs 30 kilos and was . . .

Composition

Write a short paragraph on 'Gold as a measure of value today'.

Lesson 41

Help!

A wedding

So we have to go too!

Narrator:	Bertie was on the road again at 3.15. He decided to drive to Bournemouth through Winchester.
Vicki:	I'm glad Steve and Phil came.
Bertie:	Yes. I didn't like the way that crowd looked at me. They wanted to boil me in oil.
Vicki:	Like chips!
Narrator:	At 4 o'clock they were driving through Winchester.
Eddie:	Why don't we stop for tea, dad?
Bertie:	We must get to Bournemouth. Your mother is probably there by now.
Narrator:	On the way out of Winchester, Vicki noticed the Somna was going very slowly.
Vicki:	Why don't you overtake, dad?
Eddie:	Yes, dad. I like it when you drive fast!
Bertie:	I can't. Look at the cars in front of us and behind us. They're going to a wedding.
Vicki:	So we have to go to the wedding, too!

Talk about the Story!

1   Tell us what might happen if they stopped for tea in Winchester.
2   What do you think will happen next?

Study!

1 *The zero article*
Remember, we do not use any article:
– *before the names of people and places, etc.:*
   Bertie is taking his family to Bournemouth.
– *when we make general statements with plural countable nouns:*
   Children like chips with everything. Beans are good for you.
– *when we make general statements with uncountable nouns:*
   The crowd wanted to boil Bertie in oil.
– *when we make general statements with nouns ending in **-ing**:*
   I like swimming. Swimming is my favourite sport.

2 *A/an and the*
*Remember, we use **a** or **an**:*
– *when we first mention something. After that we use **the**:*
   An old lady gave Fay a lift. The old lady asked Fay some questions.
– *when we mean **any** person, thing, etc. (not a particular one):*
   I bought a book about birds recently.
   *We use **the** when we make a particular reference:*
   The book about birds I bought recently is very good.
– *when we are saying what someone or something **is**:*
   My father is a doctor. Susie has been a good girl all afternoon.
   What's that? – It's a radio. Isn't it small!
– *when we mean **only one**:*
   Please give me an apple. I've got a new car.
   *but we DO NOT USE **one** unless we are counting:*
   Please give me one apple *(i.e. and not* two, three, *etc.)* and two oranges.

Practise!

1 *Make statements using the names of people and places, e.g.:*
   S My friend Jan lives in Amsterdam.
      Bertie is going to Bournemouth. etc.

2 *Make statements saying what kind of food you like and don't like, e.g.:*
   S I like beans. I don't like eggs.
      I like salt on my food. I don't like sugar in my tea. etc.

3 *Make general statements using the following nouns:*
   – oil, petrol, water, wheat, rice, sugar, etc., e.g.:
      S Oil is found in many parts of the world.
   – doctors, nurses, teachers, students, children, etc., e.g.:
      S Doctors have to work very hard.
   – life, truth, freedom, education, knowledge, etc., e.g.:
      S Life is just one thing after another.

4 *Tell us what people you know do for a living, e.g.:*
   S My friend Jane is a nurse.

Lesson 42

Read . . .

Not new in Nubia!

Have you ever been very ill? If so,
you will know the value of
antibiotics. We think of antibiotics as a
20th century discovery, but the
5 Nubians who lived in the Sudan over
1,500 years ago were using them too.
Scientists recently found proof of
this when examining skeletons from a
Nubian cemetery of about 450 AD.
10 These ancient people suffered very
little from infection and probably
obtained their antibiotics from
bacteria which grow on wheat and barley.
These bacteria like a dry warm climate
15 and the desert was ideal for them.

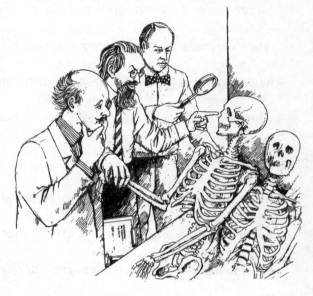

. . . they examined skeletons

. . . and Choose!

1 The use of antibiotics
a) causes infection. b) may not be as
modern as we think. c) is necessary for
growing wheat and barley.

2 Scientists decided that the Nubians
probably knew about antibiotics because
a) they grew wheat and barley. b) the
desert is warm and dry. c) the skeletons
didn't show signs of disease.

Look, Listen and Say!

*Look at the notes below while listening to the recording of a text about the story of antibiotics.
Then use these notes to tell us this story.*

1 1928 – Sir Alexander Fleming – growing bacteria on a glass plate
2 Noticed some green mould growing among bacteria
3 Mould – made a liquid – killed the bacteria
4 Fleming tried the liquid out on other bacteria – killed them too
5 Called the liquid 'penicillin'
6 Ten years later, Florey and Chain – yellow powder
7 When used on body – killed bacteria – not harm skin
8 Used it in the blood of mice – killed bacteria
9 Used it on human beings – policeman dying of infection
10 After 2nd World War – large quantities – everyone could use it

83

A Slice of Life

This is a leaflet describing a popular brand of aspirin. The information has not been simplified in any way.

Read it and explain: *– what the medicine is for, how you take it, how much you take, how often.*

Writing/Homework

Guided Summary

Read the text on page 83 again. Complete these sentences to tell us about antibiotics in ancient Nubia. Your answer should be in one paragraph of not more than 50 words.

1   Scientists believe that the Nubians . . .
2   Skeletons dating from 450 AD show . . .
3   The Nubians probably obtained . . .

Composition

Write a short paragraph giving someone advice on what they should do if they are suffering from flu.

Lesson 43

Help!

A funeral

So we have to go too!

Narrator:	At 4.30 Fay got a lift in a big black Rolls Royce. The driver was a very rich and very nice old gentleman on his way to Bournemouth. The car moved quickly and quietly through the streets of Winchester.
Man:	What's that?
Fay:	Oh, just a jar of coffee. I enjoy a cup of coffee now and again and always carry a jar with me.
Man:	Good. Let's have a cup.
Narrator:	The man pressed a button and two minutes later a tray appeared. On it were cups, milk and a pot of hot water.
Fay:	Amazing! Who does the washing up?
Man:	There's a dishwasher on the left.
Narrator:	As she made the coffee, Fay noticed the car was going very slowly and she wanted to know why.
Man:	I can't overtake. Look at the cars in front of us and behind us. They're going to a funeral.
Fay:	So we have to go to the funeral, too!

Talk about the Story!

1 Where were Bertie and the children when Fay was going to a funeral? There have been some coincidences in the story — something happens to one character and then nearly the same thing happens to another. Tell us about these events.
2 What do you think will happen next?

85

Study!

NECESSITY: 'A scale of choice'
We can express necessity on 'a scale of choice'. At one end of the scale, in the opinion of the speaker, there is some choice; at the other end of the scale, there is no choice at all:

should: You should see a doctor.
        = In my opinion, it is advisable.

ought to: You ought to see a doctor.
        = In my opinion, it is advisable.
        Ought to *is sometimes a little stronger than* **should**.

had better: You had better see a doctor.
        = I strongly recommend this.
        We often use **had better** *in warnings and threats.*

have to: You have to see a doctor.
        = In my opinion, you have no choice.
        We can normally use **have to** *in place of* **must**. *When we want to refer to the past, we use* **had to** *because there is no past form of* **must**.

have got to: You have got to see a doctor.
        = In my opinion, you have no choice.
        This is the same as **have to**, *but more informal.*

must: You must see a doctor.
        = In my opinion, you have no choice.

Practise!

stay in bed
drink a lot of water
eat very little
take some medicine
stay warm
call a doctor

You friend is ill in bed. Make statements according to 'a scale of choice':
S   You should stay in bed.
or   You ought to stay in bed.
or   You had better stay in bed.
or   You have to stay in bed.
or   You have got to stay in bed.
or   You must stay in bed.

Lesson 44

Read . . .

A genius without a brain?

Jeremy Taylor looks quite normal. He
has an IQ of 126 and has just obtained
a degree in maths. But a doctor noticed
that Jeremy's head looked slightly
5 larger than normal. A brain scan showed
that the *mantle* of the young man's
brain was 1mm thick instead of the usual
4.5mm. Jeremy's brain was very small
and his head was mainly full of water!
10 Doctors are beginning to doubt that there
is any connection between the size of a
person's brain and his intelligence.
There's hope for us all!

. . . his head was mainly full of water!

. . . and Complete!

1 A doctor noticed that the . . . of Jeremy's
head was larger than normal.
2 The . . . of the mantle was only 1mm.

3 Doctors have some . . . whether the size of
a person's brain is . . . with how . . . he is.

Listen and Do!

*Cover all the pictures below at once. We're going to make the brain do some work. You will
need a piece of paper to cover the pictures while we're doing this experiment. You will also
need a pencil. Now listen and follow the instructions.*

A 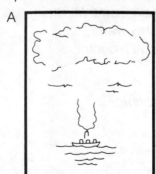   B 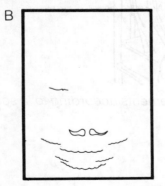   C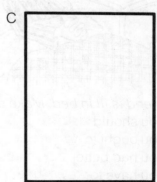

Now you give the instructions and explain what the brain was trying to do.

A Slice of Life

Here is a test which was recently given to school leavers in Britain.

Do the test as quickly as you can. Write the answers in your notebook.
Which are the easiest/hardest questions? Is the test as a whole easy or difficult?

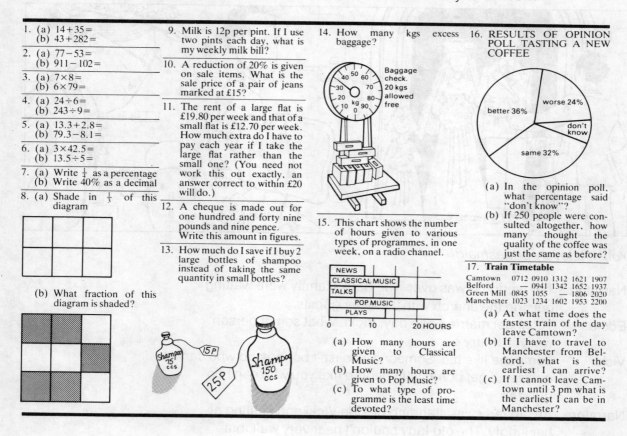

1. (a) $14 + 35 =$
   (b) $43 + 282 =$
2. (a) $77 - 53 =$
   (b) $911 - 102 =$
3. (a) $7 \times 8 =$
   (b) $6 \times 79 =$
4. (a) $24 \div 6 =$
   (b) $243 \div 9 =$
5. (a) $13.3 + 2.8 =$
   (b) $79.3 - 8.1 =$
6. (a) $3 \times 42.5 =$
   (b) $13.5 \div 5 =$
7. (a) Write $\frac{1}{4}$ as a percentage
   (b) Write 40% as a decimal
8. (a) Shade in $\frac{1}{3}$ of this diagram
   (b) What fraction of this diagram is shaded?

9. Milk is 12p per pint. If I use two pints each day, what is my weekly milk bill?

10. A reduction of 20% is given on sale items. What is the sale price of a pair of jeans marked at £15?

11. The rent of a large flat is £19.80 per week and that of a small flat is £12.70 per week. How much extra do I have to pay each year if I take the large flat rather than the small one? (You need not work this out exactly, an answer correct to within £20 will do.)

12. A cheque is made out for one hundred and forty nine pounds and nine pence. Write this amount in figures.

13. How much do I save if I buy 2 large bottles of shampoo instead of taking the same quantity in small bottles?

14. How many kgs excess baggage?

Baggage check.
20 kgs allowed free

15. This chart shows the number of hours given to various types of programmes, in one week, on a radio channel.

NEWS
CLASSICAL MUSIC
TALKS
POP MUSIC
PLAYS

0   10   20 HOURS

(a) How many hours are given to Classical Music?
(b) How many hours are given to Pop Music?
(c) To what type of programme is the least time devoted?

16. RESULTS OF OPINION POLL TASTING A NEW COFFEE

worse 24%
better 36%
don't know
same 32%

(a) In the opinion poll, what percentage said "don't know"?
(b) If 250 people were consulted altogether, how many thought the quality of the coffee was just the same as before?

17. **Train Timetable**

Camtown	0712	0910	1312	1621	1907
Belford	—	0941	1342	1652	1937
Green Mill	0845	1055	—	1806	2020
Manchester	1023	1234	1602	1953	2200

(a) At what time does the fastest train of the day leave Camtown?
(b) If I have to travel to Manchester from Belford, what is the earliest I can arrive?
(c) If I cannot leave Camtown until 3 pm what is the earliest I can be in Manchester?

Writing/Homework

Guided Summary

Read the text on page 87 again. Complete these sentences to tell us about the brain. Your answer should be in one paragraph of not more than 55 words.

1   Though Jeremy Taylor, with an IQ of 126, looks quite normal, the mantle . . .
2   Because Jeremy's head is mainly full of water, doctors . . .

Composition

Write about the test in A Slice of Life above. Say which questions you think are easy or difficult and why, and whether you think the kinds of problems set would be useful in everyday life.

Lesson 45

Help!

The wedding

You're a lovely bridesmaid!

Narrator: The wedding was over. The Banks family were waiting outside the church with the other guests.

Eddie: You'll get married one day, Vicki. What sort of person will you marry?

Vicki: Someone like me. Someone who isn't boring and who can do quizzes. I get bored with people like you who can't do quizzes.

Narrator: An old lady was standing beside Vicki and smiling at her kindly. The old lady couldn't hear very well, but she spoke to Vicki.

Old lady: Such a sweet child! Are you a bridesmaid, dear?

Vicki: No, are you?

Old lady: Pardon?

Vicki: I said, 'How are you?'.

Old lady: Oh, very well, thank you dear.

Vicki: Can you do this quiz?

Old lady: So your name is Liz. What a lovely name! You're a lovely bridesmaid, Liz!

Talk about the Story!

1 What's your opinion of Vicki and Eddie?
2 Tell us about the children's behaviour starting from the beginning of the story up to the present.

89

Study!

1   **Get** + *adjective*
We can use **get** *in the sense of* **become** *with some adjectives, such as* **annoyed, bored, depressed, ill, nervous, tired, upset,** *etc.*
How did you **get ill** when you were on holiday?
It's nothing to **get upset** about.

2   **Get** + *past participle*
We can use **get** *in place of* **be** *with a few past participles like the following:* **arrested, burnt, caught, confused, delayed, divorced, dressed, hurt, killed, lost, married** *and* **stuck:**
I often **get lost** when I'm in a strange city.
I **got lost** when I visited London.
Please come with me, or I'll **get lost.**

Practise!

1   S1 Don't get annoyed!
    S2 I'll try not to.

annoyed
bored
depressed
ill
nervous
tired
upset

2   S1 Mind you don't get caught!
    S2 I'll try not to!

caught
delayed
killed
lost
stuck

3   S1 What happened to you?
    S2 I got caught in the traffic

caught in the traffic
confused by the road signs
delayed in Vienna
hurt in an accident
lost in the city
stuck in a lift

Lesson 46

Read . . .

Robots

Robots have been used in the car
industry for some time. They can paint,
weld, learn and remember. They don't
ask for more pay and can work 24 hours
5 a day. More advanced robots can feel,
see, grasp and walk. How do they work?
Through microprocessors, of course.
Vision is provided by linking a TV
camera to a microprocessor. Hearing
10 comes from a voice recognition unit
which can understand a number of words
and phrases. A robot, nicknamed Snoopy,
has been designed to replace dogs for
the blind.

A robot nicknamed Snoopy . . .

. . . and Interpret!

1 What do you understand by the sentence 'They don't ask for more pay and can work 24 hours a day'?

2 What are the 'eyes' and 'ears' of some robots?

3 How do you think the robot learns to understand words and phrases?

Look, Listen and Say!

You are listening to a talk about robots with 'slides'.

1 *Look at the pictures below and listen.*

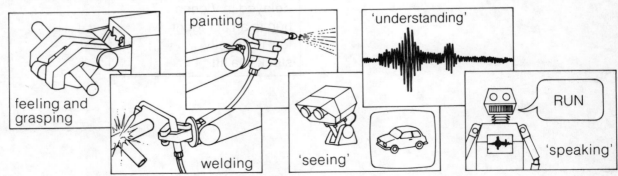

2 *Now look at the pictures and give the talk yourself.*

A Slice of Life

Here is a selection of robots.

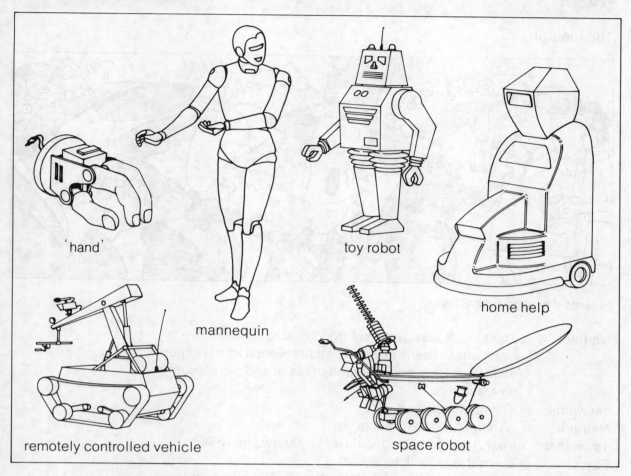

'hand'

mannequin

toy robot

home help

remotely controlled vehicle

space robot

Say how you think they are used and talk about possible future developments.

Writing/Homework

Guided Summary

Read the text on page 91 again. Complete these sentences to tell us about robots. Your answer should be in one paragraph of not more than 45 words.

1 In the car industry, robots . . .
2 More developed robots . . .
3 They work . . . and can 'see' with . . . and 'hear' . . .

Composition

Basing your answer on A Slice of Life above, write two or three paragraphs about robots.

Lesson 47

Help!

The funeral

He was a wonderful hatmaker.

Narrator:	The funeral was over. Fay stood next to the old gentleman. Then she noticed there were a lot of women all round. They were dressed in black and were wearing fantastic hats.
1st woman:	Very sad, very sad,
Narrator:	. . . said a woman next to Fay.
1st woman:	Poor Alphonse Chapeau! Did you know him well?
Fay:	Er – not very well, really.
1st woman:	Alphonse was a wonderful hatmaker. We all bought our hats from him and I don't know what we'll do now. Where's your hat, my dear?
Fay:	Er – I think I left it in the car.
1st woman:	In the car? You should wear it all the time! You shouldn't go anywhere without your hat!
2nd woman:	Who's going to make our hats now?
Narrator:	. . . said another woman, with tears in her eyes. She began to cry loudly. Soon all the women in the crowd were crying as they thought about poor Alphonse. And Fay cried too!

Talk about the Story!

1 Why is Fay embarrassed when she is asked if she knew Alphonse well?
2 Fay is still carrying her jar of coffee. Tell us about this jar from the beginning to the present.

Study!

INADVISABILITY → PROHIBITION: *'A scale of choice'*
We can say that something isn't advisable at one end of a scale. This means that, in the opinion of the speaker, there is a choice. At the other end of the scale, we can say that something is forbidden. This means that, in the opinion of the speaker, there is no choice at all:

shouldn't: You shouldn't get up today.
= In my opinion, it is not advisable.

oughtn't to: You oughtn't to get up today.
= In my opinion, it is your duty not to get up.
Oughtn't to *is sometimes a little stronger than* **shouldn't.**

had better not: You had better not get up today.
= I strongly recommend this.
We often use **had better not** *in warnings and threats.*

can't: You can't get up today.
= I forbid you to get up today.
This use of **can't** *means 'not allowed to' and is as strong as* **mustn't**. *In the opinion of the speaker there is no choice.*

mustn't: You mustn't get up today.
= I forbid you to get up today.
In the opinion of the speaker there is no choice.

Practise!

get up today
talk very much
eat very much
go to work for a week
try to read or watch TV
upset yourself

Your friend is ill in bed. Make statements according to 'a scale of choice':
S   You shouldn't get up today.
or   You oughtn't to get up today.
or   You had better not get up today.
or   You can't get up today.
or   You mustn't get up today.

Lesson 48

Read . . .

7,000 men

In 1974 some farmers were digging a
well near Xianyang in the Shanxi
province in China, when they made the
greatest archaeological discovery of the
5 century. Eight metres down, there were
7,000 life-size clay figures with
weapons and horses. They had lain there
since the time of the emperor, Chin
Shih Huang (221–206 BC) He was the
10 emperor who completed the Great Wall of
China. Before his time, servants and
horses were buried alive when the
emperor died. Chin Shih broke with this
custom and had clay figures instead.

. . . clay figures with weapons and horses

. . . and Choose!

1 The farmers who made this discovery
   a) knew about the clay figures. b) were
   trying to get water. c) were working for
   archaeologists.

2 The action of Chin Shih Huang
   a) saved many lives. b) caused many
   deaths. c) was not unusual.

Listen and Answer!

You are going to hear the story of the Great Wall of China.

1 *Listen and then answer the questions below:*
   1 About how long is the Great Wall of China?
   2 How did the Great Wall begin?
   3 What did the Emperor Chin Shih Huang do when he made China one united country?
   4 What part of China does the Great Wall cross?
   5 About how old are the parts of the wall we can see today?
   6 How was the wall used to send messages about enemy attacks?
   7 About how far north of Beijing can you see the Great Wall?
   8 How wide is the wall?
   9 What can you see every few hundred metres?
   10 What can you think of as you stand on the wall?

2 *Now look at the questions above and tell us about the Great Wall of China.*

A Slice of Life

Read this amazing story, then ask and answer questions about it. Then tell the story.

SAVE THE KING!

- In 1963 at Abu Simbel the water of the Nile's new Aswan Dam was rising quickly. The temples and three great statues of Rameses II were in danger.

- A Swedish firm made a plan to save the 3,200-year-old treasures.

- Engineers cut the temples and statues into 1,050 pieces. They moved 330,000 tons of rock higher up.

- The work took four and a half years and cost £16,666,666!

- Now Rameses II looks across Lake Nasser.

Writing/Homework

Guided Summary

Read the text on page 95 again. Complete these sentences to tell us about the 7,000 figures. Your answer should be in one paragraph of not more than 40 words.

1 In 1974 some farmers who . . . found . . . eight metres down.
2 They had been buried with . . . who . . .

Composition

WITHOUT LOOKING at the text in A Slice of Life above, write the story of Abu Simbel in your own words.

Lesson 49

Help!

Bournemouth at last!

I'd like an ice-cream please.

Bertie: Bournemouth at last!
Eddie: Where are we going to find our mum now?
Bertie: Well, it's only six o'clock, Eddie. We can walk round
           till we find her.
Vicki: Let's go to the beach.
Bertie: Just a minute. Where are we?
Narrator: Bertie looked at the map.
Bertie: Here we are. Albert Road. We're near the Town Hall. This
           must be the centre of Bournemouth.
Narrator: They left the Somna and walked along the Promenade.
           Then they went down to the beach.
Vicki: Look at all these people. Most of them are tourists like
           us. They're having a holiday or looking for their
           mothers. Look, there's an ice-cream van. Dad, I'd like
           an ice-cream. Vanilla please.
Eddie: I'd like one, too, please. Chocolate.
Bertie: I think I'll have strawberry.

Talk about the Story!

1   How do you think they will meet Fay?
2   What do you think they will do after they find her?

Study!

Here *and* there

1   **Here** *tells us where something is when it is NEAR the speaker;* **there** *tells us where something is when it is AT A DISTANCE from the speaker:*
This is my house, here. That is my house, there.

2   *We often use phrases with* **here** *and* **there** *when we are offering something:*
Here's your coffee/There's your coffee. *(You are offering it or indicating.)*
Where's my coffee? – Here you are/There you are.
Where's my coffee? – Here it is/There it is.

3   *We often use phrases with* **here** *and* **there** *to show ARRIVAL:*
Here we are in Bournemouth at last! (= We have arrived!)
Where's Bertie? – Here he is. (= He has just arrived/I have just seen him.)
Where are Bertie and the children? – Here they are. (= They have just arrived.)
Where's Bertie? – There he is. *(at a distance)*
Where are Bertie and the children? – There they are. *(at a distance)*

4   *We often use* **Here's the** *. . . and* **There's the** *. . . to say that something we are expecting has arrived or is arriving:*
Here's the bus. (It's arrived.)   There's the bus. (It's arriving.)
We use **Here's a** *. . . and* **There's a** *. . . for something we are not expecting:*
Here's a bus. Let's catch it.
There's an ice-cream van. Let's get an ice-cream.
Do not confuse this use of **There's** *with* **There is/There's** *to show EXISTENCE.*
There's a bus every half hour.   There's a bus-stop near my house.

Practise!

1   *Using objects in the classroom, practise offering or indicating with* **here** *and* **there**:
S1 Where's my book?
S2 Here you are. *(or* Here it is.*) (i.e. near)*
      There you are. *(or* There it is.*) (i.e. at a distance)*
S1 Where are my books?
S2 Here you are. *(or* Here they are.*)*
      There you are. *(or* There they are.*)*

2   *Refer to people in the classroom and practise indicating them with* **here** *and* **there**:
S1 Where's Eric?
S2 Here he is. *(i.e. near) or* There he is. *(i.e. at a distance)*
S1 Where are Eric and Jane?
      Here they are. *or* There they are.

3   *You have just seen someone or something arriving that you are not expecting. Practise statements with* **there**:
S There's Eric! There's our teacher! There's a bus! There's a taxi! etc.

Lesson 50

Read . . .

Heaven and Earth

If you stand in the Sistine Chapel and
look up, you cannot see very much of
Michelangelo's great masterpiece. To
help us, the famous Japanese photogra-
5 pher, Takashi Okamura, has photographed
the whole ceiling, section by section.
He has published 400 colour plates —
100 of them the same size as the original
paintings. He worked on scaffolding and
10 described his experience in his diary:
'I can see even the smallest traces of
Michelangelo's brush . . . I can even see
thin spiders' webs. Even being in this
uncomfortable position, I wondered what
15 the spiders lived on — such a foolish
thought came up.'

He worked on scaffolding . . .

. . . and Answer!

1 Why did Takashi Okamura take 400 colour
plates of the Sistine Chapel?
2 How did he get near enough to the
paintings to photograph them?

3 Why do you think he describes his thought
about the spiders as 'foolish'?

Look, Listen and Take Notes!

You are going to hear a talk about Michelangelo and the picture below.

1 *Listen and take notes.*

2 *Refer to your notes and give the talk you have just heard.*

99

A Slice of Life

Here are some simple instructions on taking a photograph.

Study the instructions, then
1   *Ask and answer questions about them.*
2   *Tell us how to take a photograph, step by step.*

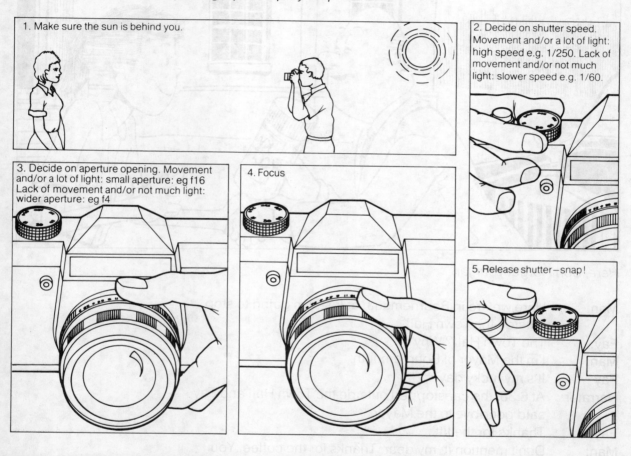

1. Make sure the sun is behind you.

2. Decide on shutter speed. Movement and/or a lot of light: high speed e.g. 1/250. Lack of movement and/or not much light: slower speed e.g. 1/60.

3. Decide on aperture opening. Movement and/or a lot of light: small aperture: eg f16 Lack of movement and/or not much light: wider aperture: eg f4

4. Focus

5. Release shutter – snap!

Writing/Homework

Guided Summary

Read the text on page 99 again. Complete these sentences to tell us about Takashi Okamura. Your answer should be in one paragraph of not more than 30 words.

1   The famous Japanese photographer, Takashi Okamura, has photographed . . .
2   He has published 400 . . . which show . . .

Composition

WITHOUT LOOKING at the information in A Slice of Life above, write instructions on how to take a photograph.

Lesson 51

Help!

Bournemouth at last!

Here, don't forget your jar.

Man:	Here we are in Bournemouth at last! I'm going to stop outside the Town Hall.
Fay:	The Town Hall? Why?
Man:	I'm the Mayor of Bournemouth.
Fay:	It's my lucky day!
Narrator:	At 6.30, the car stopped outside the Town Hall and Fay said goodbye to the Mayor.
Fay:	Thanks for the lift.
Man:	Don't mention it, my dear. Thanks for the coffee. You make excellent coffee. Here, don't forget your jar.
Fay:	Now I wonder where I'm going to find that husband of mine and where I'm going to find my children,
Narrator:	. . . Fay thought as she walked along Bourne Avenue. When she came to The Square, Fay bought a newspaper. She walked up Richmond Hill and turned right into Albert Road. As she walked, she read her paper.
Fay:	I wonder what The Stars say.

Talk about the Story!

1 'It's my lucky day.' How has Fay been lucky today?
2 What's going to happen next?

Study!

Reporting verbs

1   *The most common 'reporting verbs' which we use in indirect speech are* **say** *and* **tell (me)** *(for statements), and* **ask (me)** *for questions. We use these verbs when we are reporting to another person what someone else said or asked:*
Bertie **said** he was going to look for somewhere to park the car.
Bertie **told me** he was going to look for somewhere to park the car.
Bertie **asked (me)** if there was anywhere he could park the car.
Bertie **asked (me)** where he could park the car.

2   *We often use 'reporting verbs' even if we are not reporting something to someone else. For example, we may be 'thinking':*
I **wonder** where Bertie is.

3   *If we are reporting Yes/No questions, we use* **if** *or* **whether** *after the verb:*

Yes/No Question: Is Bertie here?
Reporting Verb: I **wonder if** (or **whether**) Bertie is here.
                      Do you **know**/I don't **know if** (or **whether**) Bertie is here.

Wh-Question: Where is Bertie?
Reporting Verb: I **wonder where** Bertie is. (**where** + *subject* + *verb*)
                      Do you **know where**/I don't **know where**/I **know where** Bertie is.

Practise!

Put yourself in Fay's position and report her thoughts:

Is Bertie here?
Are they far away?
Have they all arrived?
Will I find them?
Can I find them?

S   I wonder if Bertie is here
or   I don't know if Bertie is here.

Where is Bertie?
Where are Bertie and the children?
When did they arrive?
How will I find them?
Why aren't they here?

S   I wonder where Bertie is.
or   I don't know where Bertie is.

Lesson 52

Read . . .

Heathrow: some facts

If you're ever in London's Heathrow
Airport, look around you before your
flight is called. About 60,000 people
work there. The airport covers an area
5 of 1,140.8 hectares and is used by 30
million passengers a year. Vehicles enter
the airport at the rate of 40,000 an
hour. About 1,000 planes fly in and out
every day in the summer. Among the many
10 different buildings, there's a hostel

'Ark of the Air'

for animals, nicknamed 'Ark of the Air'.
Millions of animals have been through
it since it opened in 1962. To put it
mildly, Heathrow is a busy place!

. . . and Answer!

All numbers should be written as words not as figures in your answers.

1 How many people work in Heathrow?
2 How many hectares does the airport
cover?

3 How many vehicles enter the airport each
hour?
4 How many planes fly in and out every day
in the summer?

Listen and Decide!

*You are looking at a departure board at Heathrow Airport, London. You will hear eight flight
announcements, numbered 1 to 8. Write the number of each announcement against its
position on the board below. The first one has been done for you:*

DEPARTURES				
KLM	464	Amsterdam	Gate 12	
OA	363	Athens	Gate 14	
SABENA	470	Brussels	Gate 19	1
LH	204	Frankfurt	Gate 22	
OS	616	Vienna		
IB	703	Madrid		
AF	519	Paris		
AIR ITALIA	406	Rome		

A Slice of Life

Here are some of the signs and symbols you would see at London's Heathrow Airport.

Ask and answer:

1 S1 (e.g.): What sign should I look for if I want to buy some tax-free goods?
  S2 You should look for Number 6, Duty Free Goods

2 S1 What's Number 6?
  S2 It's Duty Free Goods. It means . . . (*give the word(s) in your own language*)

Writing/Homework

Guided Summary

Read the text on page 103 again. Complete these sentences to tell us about Heathrow. Your answer should be in one paragraph of not more than 50 words.

1 London's Heathrow Airport is very large (it covers . . .) and very busy (it is used . . .)
2 As many as 40,000 . . . and in the summer about . . .

Composition

Imagine you have just arrived in Heathrow and are going to be met by some English friends. Describe what you have to do from the moment the plane lands to the moment you greet your friends.

Lesson 53

Help!

Your lucky stars

Look up! Your troubles are over!

Narrator:	While they were on the beach, Eddie suddenly remembered something.
Eddie:	Dad, you haven't locked the Somna.
Bertie:	You're right, Eddie. Let's go and lock it.
Eddie:	Please let me lock it, dad.
Vicki:	No one wants to steal *that*!
Narrator:	Meanwhile, Fay was walking along Albert Road, reading YOUR LUCKY STARS.
Fay:	'Little things will give you a lot of headaches today.' Mm. That's certainly happened.
Narrator:	Fay remembered Bertie's newspaper and looked at the jar of coffee.
Fay:	'Money will come to you from friendly strangers.' Yes, and it was very nice. 'Don't leave home without a hat.' How true! I certainly needed a hat today! Poor Alphonse! 'Look up! Your troubles are nearly over!'
Narrator:	Fay looked up and there, in front of her, was the Somna!
Fay:	Heavens! Our Somna!

Talk about the Story!

1   What do you think is going to happen next?
2   The Somna is like a 'character' in the story. Tell us about its adventures today.

Study!

Let

1   *We use the imperative form* **let's** *when we are making suggestions for ourselves with other people. We may use it on its own:*
Let's go for a swim.   – Yes, let's!
or with . . . **shall we?**:
Let's go for a swim, **shall we**? – No, I'd rather not!
The affirmative reply to suggestions is often: **Yes, let's.**
The negative reply to suggestions is often: **No, I'd rather not.**
The negative of **Let's** *is* **Don't let's** *or* **Let's not**:
Don't let's (*or* **Let's not**) go for a swim. **Let's** go fishing instead.

2   *We can also use* **let** *as an ordinary irregular verb* (**let – let – let**) *meaning 'allow'. The verb* **let** *is never followed by* **to**. *We can use it in the imperative:*
Let me **help** you. (= Allow me to help you.)
and we can use it in all tenses:
I won't **let** anyone **drive** my car.
Fay **doesn't let** her children **watch** TV till they have done their homework.
Fay **didn't let** Vicki **go** to a party yesterday.

3   *We do not normally use* **let** (= allow) *in the Passive. We have to use* **(not) allowed to** *instead:* No one is **allowed to drive** my car. Vicki **wasn't allowed** to go.

Practise!

walk on the grass   swim here   camp here

1   S1 Let's walk on the grass
    S2 We can't.
    S1 Why not?
    S2 They won't let us.
        That sign says KEEP OFF THE
        GRASS

2   S1 Let's walk on the grass
    S2 We can't. We're not allowed to.
        That sign says KEEP OFF THE
        GRASS

3   S1 They won't let us walk on the grass
    S2 How do you know?
    S1 That sign says KEEP OFF THE
        GRASS

4   S1 We're not allowed to walk on the
        grass
    S2 How do you know?
    S1 That sign says KEEP OFF THE
        GRASS

Lesson 54

Read . . .

Newspapers

Newspapers are now produced cheaply
using computers. First, journalists
type their stories directly on to
computers. Then a larger computer
5 'arranges' the stories to fit the page
design. The material is then fed into
a machine called a phototypesetter,
which can print 4,000 lines per minute.
After that, another computer is used

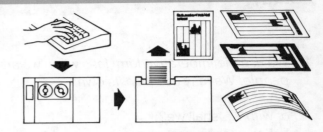

. . . use of computers and photo-typesetters

10 to combine words and pictures. The
page is then finished. A negative
is made of the page and a plate (made
of polymer) is made from the negative.
The page is now ready for printing.

. . . and Interpret!

1 Give some reasons why the method
described in the text for printing
newspapers is cheaper than other
methods.

2 Tell us what you know about older
methods for printing newspapers and
describe how they compare with the
methods described in the text.

Look, Listen and Say!

'SHOULD WE ALWAYS USE NEW METHODS FOR MAKING THINGS?'
1 *Listen to the arguments FOR and AGAINST while looking at the notes below.*
2 *Use the notes and other ideas to talk about the subject in class.*

FOR	AGAINST
1 Always been fight – new methods and old	Seem to be saying – machines more important than people
2 We are always looking – cheaper methods: newspapers, anything	Always new methods making or doing things – don't have to use them
3 Cheaper methods – people out of jobs	Farm – expensive machine = 20 people
4 New methods – new and different jobs – save people hard work	Better employ 20 people – than use the new machine
5 Can't pretend new methods don't exist	People – right to work
6 If we don't use them – others will – make cheaper goods – put us out of business	New methods take this right away – thousands out of work – kind of society we want?

A Slice of Life

Here are the names of four well-known British newspapers:

Supply the names of four well-known papers published daily in this country:

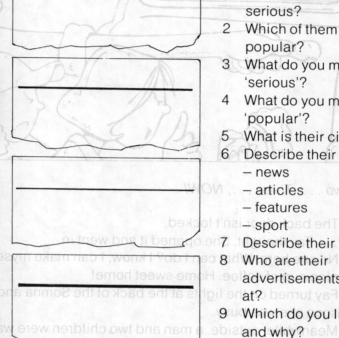

Discuss the following questions about the newspapers you have chosen:

1 Which of them are serious?
2 Which of them are popular?
3 What do you mean by 'serious'?
4 What do you mean by 'popular'?
5 What is their circulation?
6 Describe their contents:
 – news
 – articles
 – features
 – sport
7 Describe their 'politics'.
8 Who are their advertisements aimed at?
9 Which do you like best and why?

Writing/Homework

Guided Summary

Read the text on page 107 again. Complete these sentences to tell us how a modern newspaper is produced. Your answer should be in one paragraph of not more than 60 words.

1 After journalists write their stories, a large computer . . .
2 The material is then fed into . . .
3 Another computer combines . . . and the page is finished.
4 The last step is to make a negative of the page and then . . .

Composition

Write two or three paragraphs about the newspaper you like best. Describe it briefly, then say why you like it.

Lesson 55

Help!

I'll make myself a nice cup of coffee.

One . . ., Two . . ., Three . . ., NOW!

Fay: The back door isn't locked,
Narrator: . . . Fay thought. She opened it and went in.
Fay: No one here. What can I do? I know, I can make myself a nice cup of coffee. Home sweet home!
Narrator: Fay turned on the lights at the back of the Somna and soon she was busy.
Meanwhile, outside, a man and two children were walking quietly round the Somna.
Eddie: Dad, there's a thief in there. The light's on and I can hear someone.
Bertie: Yes, what can we do?
Vicki: If you both listen to me, you won't get hurt! We can open the door suddenly. I'll push this ice-cream in his face. Eddie can hold his legs and you can jump on him, dad. Sh! We must be very quiet!
Narrator: They all stood in front of the back door.
Vicki: Don't move until I tell you. Wait till I count up to three. One . . ., Two . . ., Three . . ., NOW!

Talk about the Story!

1 Is this what you thought was going to happen? Tell us what you thought was going to happen.
2 Tell us about some of the things Vicki has done today.

Study!

Reflexive pronouns

1   *FORM*

myself   yourself   himself   herself   itself

ourselves   yourselves   themselves

2   *Here are some common verbs that can be followed by reflexive pronouns which refer back to the subject. They are NEVER followed by object pronouns like* **me, him, her,** *etc.):* **amuse, blame, cut, dry, enjoy** *and* **hurt.**
I **cut myself** shaving this morning.
We really **enjoyed ourselves** at the party.

3   *With verbs like* **dress, hide** *and* **wash** *we do not normally use reflexive pronouns. They are implied:*
I must **dress/wash**.   (*i.e.* 'dress/wash myself')
Let's **hide**.   (*i.e.* 'hide ourselves')

4   *Many verbs such as* **get up, sit down, stand up, wake up,** *and combinations like* **get cold, get hot, get dressed, get hurt, get married,** *etc. (Lesson 45) are not reflexive in English:*
I **got up** with difficulty this morning.

5   *We often use reflexive pronouns after* **by** *to mean 'without help':*
I made this cupboard **by myself**.
and after other prepositions:
I made a cup of coffee **for myself**. (= I **made myself** a cup of coffee.)

6   *We sometimes use reflexives for extra emphasis:*
The quiz was so hard, even **Vicki herself** couldn't do it.

Practise!

1   S1 How did he **cut** himself?
     S2 I don't know. He really **hurt** himself

he	– himself
she	– herself
they	– themselves

2   S1 What did you do when he came into the room?
     S2 I **got up**.

got up
sat down
stood up
woke up

3   S1 Did someone **make** this for you?
     S2 No, I **made** it by myself.

make
write
build
do

Lesson 56

Read . . .

The Beano

The Beano, a British comic, has been
going since 1938. It is mainly read
and enjoyed by children, but many
adults like it, too. Some of its
5 characters, like Dennis the Menace,
have become cult figures. Characters
are changed from time to time as they
'wear out'. Dennis has been popular
since 1951, but Lord Snooty has been
10 going strong since *The Beano* began.

. . . *many adults like it too*

What's the secret of its success?
'There is no message; we don't preach,'
the editor says. 'We are only looking
for a laugh.'

. . . and Choose!

1 The surprising thing about *The Beano* is
   a) that it is mainly read by adults.
   b) how long it has lasted. c) its characters.

2 The characters in *The Beano*
   a) have not changed since the magazine
   began. b) are all cult figures. c) change
   from time to time.

Listen and Spot the Differences!

*Look at the text above again. While you are reading it, listen to the recording of the listening
text. See if you can spot ten differences. Make a note of them below:*

TEXT ABOVE	LISTENING TEXT
1 _____	_____
2 _____	_____
3 _____	_____
4 _____	_____
5 _____	_____
6 _____	_____
7 _____	_____
8 _____	_____
9 _____	_____
10 _____	_____

A Slice of Life

Here is an extract from a comic featuring Dotty Auntie Dotty.

Now talk about comics.

1 Did you enjoy the above? Why/Why not?
2 Tell us about comics in this country and what you think of them.
3 Do you think comics are good or bad for children? Why?

Writing/Homework

Guided Summary

Read the text on page 111 again. Complete these sentences to tell us about **The Beano***. Your answer should be in one paragraph of not more than 50 words.*

1 *The Beano* is a British comic, first published in 1938, which is aimed at . . .
2 Two of its most famous characters are . . .
3 *The Beano* is successful because the editor's policy is . . . not to . . .

Composition

Write two or three paragraphs about comics published in this country. Say whether you think they are good or bad and why.

Lesson 57

Help!

Together again!

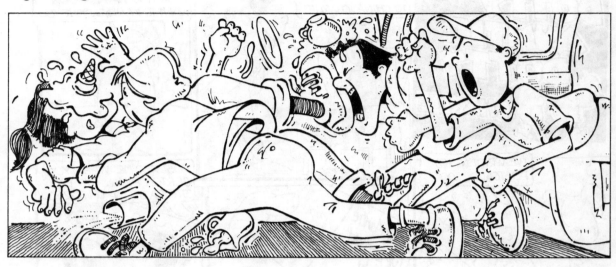

'Help!' Fay shouted.

All three:	Yaaah!
Narrator:	. . . the three of them cried as they rushed into the Somna.
Fay:	Help!
Narrator:	. . . Fay shouted. She couldn't shout any more because something cold and wet hit her face. Someone was holding her legs and someone was jumping on her. She dropped the cup of hot coffee on the man's head.
Bertie:	Help! Fire!
Narrator:	. . . the man shouted.
Vicki:	Stop! It's our mum!
Narrator:	They all sat on the floor of the Somna and looked at each other. At first they said nothing, then they all began to laugh and laugh.
Fay:	I ought to call the police,
Narrator:	. . . Fay said as she kissed them all. It took them more than an hour to tell their stories. All of them laughed and cried as they remembered the events of the day.

Talk about the Story!

1   What sorts of things did they tell each other?
2   This kind of story is called 'a farce'. Tell us about some of the comical events you can remember.

Study!

The position of **both** and **all**

1 *After* **be**

You **are both** right.   You **are all** right.
They **were both** late.   They **were all** late.

2 *After the first verb when there is more than one verb in a sentence*

You **can both swim** well.   You **can all swim** well.
They **will both be** here soon.   They **will all be** here soon.
We **have both finished** work.   We **have all finished** work.

3 *Before the main verb when there is only one verb in a sentence*

You **both heard** what he said.   You **all heard** what he said.
They **both began** to laugh.   They **all began** to laugh.

4 *Instead of saying:*   *we can say:*

You **are both** right.   **Both of you are** right.
We **have both** finished work.   **Both of us have** finished work.
We **are all** ready.   **All of us are** ready.
They **all began** to laugh.   **All of them began** to laugh.

5 *Instead of saying:*   *we can say:*

She bought **them both**.   She bought **both of them**.
She bought **them all**.   She bought **all of them**.

Practise!

1 S We are **both** ready.
   or We are **all** ready.

ready	upset
tired	ill
angry	hungry

2 S They will **both** write to you.
   or They will **all** write to you.

> will write to you
> can help you
> may see you
> must believe you
> have eaten
> have been working

3 S You **both** arrived at 5.
   or You **all** arrived at 5.

> arrived at 5
> caught the same train
> took a taxi from the station
> made the same mistake

4 *Practise some or all the above again using* Both of us, *etc.*

Lesson 58

Read . . .

Men's hair styles

In the 18th century men wore wigs to hide their baldness. In the 19th century, long hair was in fashion. 'Short back and sides' became normal at the
5 time of World War I (1914–1918). It was the standard hair style till the 1960's. Since then, anything goes: long hair, shaven heads ('skinheads'), Afro hair styles and perms. Barbers, who will
10 give you an old-fashioned haircut for a modest sum, co-exist with 'Gentlemen's Hair Stylists' who specialize in high fashion and charge the earth.

. . . wigs to hide their baldness

. . . and Choose!

1 In the 18th century men more wigs
a) because long hair was in fashion.
b) when they lost their hair. c) to hide their hair.

2 Since the 1960's men prefer a) short back and sides. b) long hair. c) any hair style.

Look, Listen and Say!

You're going to hear two sets of instructions. Look at the pictures below and take notes while you listen. Then use your notes to give these instructions.

Magnetic figure preserver for the middle-aged

Bathroom exercise machine for training the legs for running to the station in the morning

A Slice of Life

Here is a selection of men's and women's styles of clothing.

Say what you think of them, which you prefer and why.

Writing/Homework

Guided Summary

Read the text on page 115 again. Complete these sentences to tell us about men's hair styles. Your answer should be in one paragraph of not more than 50 words.

1   Men hid their baldness in the 18th century by . . .
2   Though long hair was in fashion in . . . , 'short back and sides' . . .
3   Since then, . . .

Composition

Basing your answer on A Slice of Life above, write two or three paragraphs about men's or women's styles of clothing, saying which style you prefer.

Lesson 59

Help!

Dinner at Leoni's

Choose the best things on the menu!

Bertie:	What shall we do now?
Vicki:	Let's go to the best restaurant in Bournemouth!
Narrator:	So, of course, they all went to Leoni's. Half an hour later, in their best clothes, they were sitting at a table in Leoni's restaurant looking at the expensive menu. Everyone looked happy except Bertie.
Bertie:	I can't afford these prices!
Narrator:	Then, Mr Leoni came to their table. He spoke to Vicki.
Mr Leoni:	Can you do quizzes, young lady?
Vicki:	Of course, I can, Mr Leoni!
Mr Leoni:	Then do this one!
Narrator:	Mr Leoni gave Vicki a quiz with ten questions in it and of course she answered every one of them correctly.
Mr Leoni:	Heavens! And I thought no one could do this quiz! You have just won free dinners for four people! Congratulations! Choose the best things on the menu!
Narrator:	And so they celebrated a happy end to a long long day!

Talk about the Story!

1 Tell us about Vicki's interest in quizzes.
2 Tell us what you liked in the story and what you didn't like.

Study!

The use of articles and apostrophe s with places

1   The bank, *etc.*

Where are you going?
I'm going to

the bank. the cinema. the theatre. the supermarket. the park.	*We often use **the** with places when we know (or think we know) which one we are referring to.*

2   A restaurant, *etc.*

Where are you going?
I'm going to

a restaurant. a friend's. a play. a film. a football match.	*We use **a/an** for places (e.g. **a restaurant**) or events (e.g. **a play**) when we don't know or we don't want to say which one we are referring to.*

3   The butcher's, *etc.*

Where are you going?
I'm going to

the butcher's. the baker's. the greengrocer's. the dentist's. the doctor's.	*We use **the** as in 1 above. But we also use apostrophe **s** after the noun to mean **shop** or **place of business**: e.g.* **butcher's shop, doctor's surgery.**

4   Leoni's, *etc.*

Where are you going?
I'm going to

Leoni's. Harridge's. my aunt's. the Robinsons'.	*i.e.* **Leoni's Restaurant** *i.e.* **Harridge's Department Store** *i.e.* **my aunt's house** *i.e.* **the Robinsons' house**

Practise!

Refer to the nouns above and practise the following exchanges:

1   S1 Where are you going?
     S2 I'm going to the bank

2   S1 Where have you been?
     S2 I've been to the bank

3   S1 Where has Bertie gone?
     S2 He's gone to the bank.

4   S1 Where are Bertie and Fay?
     S2 They're at the bank

Lesson 60

Read . . .

Eureka – again!

In 212 BC Archimedes destroyed the
Roman fleet at Syracuse with bronze
mirrors which reflected the sun's rays.
He also used steam-powered cannon. Each
5 cannon had a 5-foot wooden barrel which
fired a 22-pound stone ball as far as
3,000 feet. In our own times, a Cretan
engineer, Mr Ioannis Sakas, has tested
both these weapons successfully. Some
10 years ago, he tried out the mirrors
with the help of the Greek Navy.
Recently, Mr Sakas made a small model
of Archimedes' cannon. It worked
perfectly and fired a tennis ball filled
15 with cement over a distance of 200 feet.

Archimedes destroyed the Roman fleet.

. . . and Complete!

1 In 212 BC the Roman fleet was . . .
2 He also used cannon powered . . .
3 A 22-pound stone ball . . .

4 These weapons were . . .
5 Some years ago, the Greek Navy helped
him . . .

Listen and Answer!

You're going to hear a story about Archimedes.

1 *Listen and then answer the questions below:*
   1 Where was Archimedes born and when?
   2 Was this city Greek or Roman?
   3 Where did Archimedes study?
   4 How did he spend the rest of his life?
   5 Who was Hieron and what did he want Archimedes to tell him?
   6 What did Archimedes notice as he was getting into his bath one day?
   7 What idea did this give him?
   8 How could he tell the difference between pure gold and gold mixed with silver?
   9 What did Archimedes do when he had this idea?
   10 What does 'Eureka' mean?

2 *Now look at the questions above and tell us about Archimedes.*

A Slice of Life

Here is some information about solar heating.

Study the information, then
1 *Ask and answer questions about it.*
2 *Tell us how the system works.*
3 *Tell us about the advantages of solar heating.*

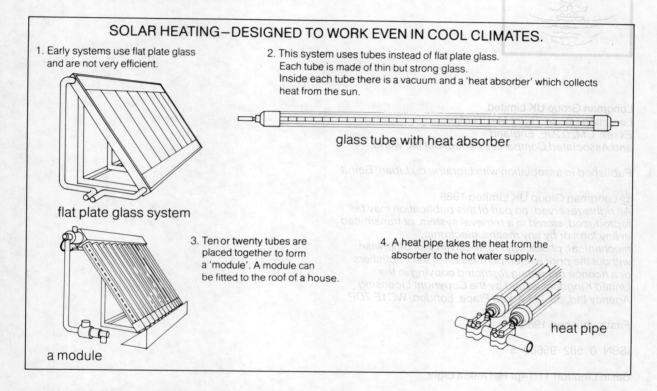

SOLAR HEATING—DESIGNED TO WORK EVEN IN COOL CLIMATES.

1. Early systems use flat plate glass and are not very efficient.

flat plate glass system

2. This system uses tubes instead of flat plate glass. Each tube is made of thin but strong glass. Inside each tube there is a vacuum and a 'heat absorber' which collects heat from the sun.

glass tube with heat absorber

3. Ten or twenty tubes are placed together to form a 'module'. A module can be fitted to the roof of a house.

a module

4. A heat pipe takes the heat from the absorber to the hot water supply.

heat pipe

Writing/Homework

Guided Summary

Read the text on page 119 again. Complete these sentences to tell us about Archimedes' weapons and Mr Sakas' tests. Your answer should be in one paragraph of not more than 55 words.

1 In 212 BC Archimedes used the sun's rays to . . .
2 He also used cannon which could . . .
3 Both these weapons were tested . . . and they . . .

Composition

WITHOUT LOOKING at the text in A Slice of Life above, write two paragraphs in your own words about solar heating.

D

Longman Group UK Limited,
Longman House, Burnt Mill, Harlow,
Essex, CM20 2JE, England
and Associated Companies throughout the world.

Published in association with Librairie du Liban, Beirut.

First published 1989

ISBN 0 582 95600 5

Set in Linotron 11/14pt Helvetica Light

Produced by Longman Group (FE) Ltd
Printed in Hong Kong

Acknowledgements

We are grateful to Faber and Faber Ltd and Harcourt Brace Jovanovich, Inc. for permission to reproduce 'Memory' by Trevor Nunn after T.S. Eliot in *Cats: The Book of The Musical* (based on *Old Possum's Book of Practical Cats* by T.S. Eliot) copyright © 1981, 1983 by Faber and Faber Limited and The Really Useful Company Limited; lyrics by Trevor Nunn incorporating lines from 'Rhapsody on a Windy Night' in *Collected Poems* 1909–1962 by T.S. Eliot, copyright 1936 by Harcourt Brace Jovanovich, Inc., copyright © 1963, 1964 by T.S. Eliot.

The Publishers are grateful to the following for their permission to reproduce photographs:–

City of Edinburgh Museums and Galleries Design Section for page 95; Daily Express for page 108; Daily Mirror Newspapers Ltd. for page 108; Gerald Duckworth & Co. Ltd. for page 115; The Guardian Newspaper Ltd. for page 108; Independent Television Publications Ltd. for page 4; Institute of Mathematics and its Applications Bulletin vol. 14, no. 4 April 1978 for page 88; Mr. Erik Liebermann for page 24; Mitchell Library, State Library of New South Wales, Australia for page 80; Nicholas Laboratories Ltd. for page 84; Photo Source for page 32; Picturepoint Ltd. for pages 23 and 99; Routledge and Kegan Paul for pages 87 and 121; Sonnenberg International for page 56; Times Newspapers Ltd. for page 108 and Topham Picture Library for page 7.

The photographs on page 44 are Longman Group copyright.